Edexcel AS Music Technology Revision Guide

EDEXCEL

Chris Duffill and Jonny Martin

R· RHINEGOLD
EDUCATION

www.rhinegoldeducation.co.uk

Music Study Guides

GCSE, AS and A2 Music Study Guides (AQA, Edexcel and OCR)

GCSE, AS and A2 Music Listening Tests (AQA, Edexcel and OCR)

AS/A2 Music Technology Study Guide (Edexcel)

AS/A2 Music Technology Listening Tests (Edexcel)

Revision Guides for GCSE (AQA, Edexcel and OCR), AS and A2 Music (AQA and Edexcel)

Also available from Rhinegold Education

Key Stage 3 Listening Tests: Book 1 and Book 2

AS and A2 Music Harmony Workbooks

GCSE and AS Music Composition Workbooks

GCSE and AS Music Literacy Workbooks

Musicals in Focus, Romanticism in Focus, Baroque Music in Focus, Film Music in Focus, Modernism in Focus, *The Immaculate Collection* in Focus, *Who's Next* in Focus, *Batman* in Focus, *Goldfinger* in Focus

Music Technology from Scratch

Dictionary of Music in Sound

First published 2011 in Great Britain by

Rhinegold Education

14–15 Berners Street

London W1T 3LJ

www.rhinegoldeducation.co.uk

© 2011 Rhinegold Education

a division of Music Sales Limited

You should always check the current requirements of the examination, since these may change. Copies of the Edexcel specification can be downloaded from the Edexcel website at www.edexcel.com. Edexcel Publications telephone: 01623 467467, fax: 01623 450481, email: publication.orders@edexcel.com.

Edexcel AS Music Technology Revision Guide

Order No. RHG329

ISBN: 978-1-907447-13-6

Exclusive Distributors:

Music Sales Ltd

Distribution Centre, Newmarket Road

Bury St Edmunds, Suffolk IP33 3YB, UK

Printed in the EU

Introduction

This book is designed to supplement [...]
Guide (2nd edition), helping to prepa[...]
and Analysing. The information in th[...]
practical work, but its main function [...]

In your examination you will be faced [...]
types of responses. There is a section [...]
examination itself and what the exan [...]
a section of revision tips, giving you 1 [...]
so you can test yourself on what you [...]

There will be questions in the exam a [...]
music through the 20th century and [...]
of the most important electronic inst [...]
You may be a guitarist with a good k [...]
section that will help you identify the [...]
be able to hear them.

You will be asked questions about ef [...]
production, and discussing aspects o [...]
achieve the sound you can hear. I her [...]
a vocabulary to deal with these types [...]
and their typical parameters, giving e [...]
that you can recognise the sounds wl [...]
sort of material by making the effort [...]
need to listen to these musical examp [...]

The rest of the book is dedicated to n [...]
identified through the 20th century a [...]
at the 'special focus styles'. These are [...]
your exam – the rest is very useful, bu [...]
Ensure that you have checked what tl [...]
that you can optimise your time and e [...]
researching the 'fingerprints' of the s[...]
Arrangement.

This book is designed to cover all the [...]
exam, but it is not a substitute for list [...]
find that the more you learn, the mor [...]
help you to figure out the questions y [...]
vocabulary to ask them intelligently.

The best advice that you can be given [...]
open your ears. Listen analytically to e [...]

Contents

The authors

Chris Duffill has a background
production and performance, a
musician. During the last ten ye
developing provision and integr
to A level, including work with
courses and consultancy for all
Music Technology.

Jonny Martin is Chair of Exam
teaching background includes
range of education establishme
is the author of the *Music Tech*
books written to support the d
for teachers every year as a mu
Alongside his activities in the w
schedule as a soloist and in a n

Acknowledgemen

The authors would like to thank
Rhinegold Education editorial a
Adrian Horsewood and Ben Sm

The following table lists some of the most important synths and keyboards, when they were invented and some recommended recordings you can listen to so that you will be able to recognise the sound of the instrument. It is likely that you will need to be able to identify one or two of the more recognisable vintage keyboard instruments (in addition to the piano!) in your listening exam.

THEREMIN (1920)

The theremin is not a keyboard instrument, but is played by moving the hands near one or two aerials. Never particularly popular because it is so difficult to play, the **theremin** experienced something of a revival in the 1990s by people who built them for their own use. It has a very pure sound with **portamento** always appearing between notes due to the playing technique. It is often played with a very obvious vibrato.

 Theremin can be heard on any recordings by Lydia Kavina, and many sci-fi films from the 1940s and 1950s. A theremin-like instrument can be heard on The Beach Boys' 'Good Vibrations' (from 0:26).

ONDES MARTENOT (1928)

The ondes Martenot is a keyboard instrument with the ability to produce theremin-like tones by using a ribbon underneath the keyboard. When using the keyboard itself, it has a noticeable attack and an almost trumpet-like sound. It was more popular in avant-garde classical music than in pop music.

 The trumpet-like tones can be heard from 2:58 to 3:30 on Radiohead's 'How To Disappear Completely'. The 'ethereal crooning' of the ribbon controller can be heard from 0:23–1:36 on Radiohead's 'The National Anthem'.

HAMMOND B-3 ORGAN (1954)

Originally invented as a low-cost alternative to the pipe organ, the Hammond B-3 became widely used in many pop music genres from the 1960s onwards. This **tonewheel**, **drawbar** organ is often played through a rotating **Leslie speaker** – the rotation speed can be altered, giving a chorus/phasing/tremolo effect.

 The B-3 can be heard on almost any Deep Purple track, or anything by Emerson, Lake & Palmer.

RHODES PIANO (1965)

The Rhodes piano produces a sound that sounds like a cross between a bell and a vibraphone (without vibrato). It is the classic electric piano sound and can be heard on many recordings. It is often played through effects pedals to produce a variety of effects similar to that of an electric guitar. A very similar (but slightly harsher) sound is produced by its main competitor, the Wurlitzer electric piano.

Introduction

This book is designed to supplement the Rhinegold *Edexcel AS/A2 Music Technology Study Guide* (2nd edition), helping to prepare you for your examination on Unit 2: Listening and Analysing. The information in this book will also help you with some aspects of your practical work, but its main function is to focus on the material needed for Unit 2.

In your examination you will be faced with different types of question, all requiring different types of responses. There is a section in this book that tells you what to expect in the examination itself and what the examiners really want to see in your answers. There is also a section of revision tips, giving you top ten tips for the exam, along with some questions so you can test yourself on what you have already learned.

There will be questions in the exam about electronic instruments that are used in popular music through the 20th century and beyond. This book identifies recordings in which some of the most important electronic instruments in our recent musical history have been used. You may be a guitarist with a good knowledge of guitar techniques but, if not, there is a section that will help you identify the main techniques, giving examples of where you might be able to hear them.

You will be asked questions about effects and processors – identifying their use in a full production, and discussing aspects of these units such as how they might be set up to achieve the sound you can hear. There is a section in this book that will help you develop a vocabulary to deal with these types of questions. It lists the main effects and processors and their typical parameters, giving examples of songs you can check out for yourself, so that you can recognise the sounds when you hear them again. You can only really learn this sort of material by making the effort to listen and apply what you have read, so you will need to listen to these musical examples in order to make the best use of this section.

The rest of the book is dedicated to many of the main styles of popular music that can be identified through the 20th century and beyond, with particular space given over to looking at the 'special focus styles'. These are the styles you will need to know in most detail for your exam – the rest is very useful, but you will not need to know it in so much detail. Ensure that you have checked what the special focus styles are for the year of your exam so that you can optimise your time and effort. This section is also an invaluable resource for researching the 'fingerprints' of the style you have chosen for Task 1C: Creative Sequenced Arrangement.

This book is designed to cover all the main areas you will need to know about for your exam, but it is not a substitute for listening – to your teacher and to your music! You may find that the more you learn, the more you realise you would like to learn, so this book may help you to figure out the questions you really want to ask your teacher and give you the vocabulary to ask them intelligently.

The best advice that you can be given for any Music or Music Technology course is to open your ears. Listen analytically to everything. When you hear an interesting sound in a production, try to figure out how it is made. Read magazines that include interviews with producers and engineers. Experiment with the equipment you have access to. Try to recreate some of the sounds that capture your imagination. Broaden your musical horizons and listen to things that would not automatically have been your first choice.

Perhaps you will already know much of the material in this book, so that it acts as a memory aid, focusing in on the main points needed for your exam. If not, don't worry. Read through the book, checking out the musical examples and making notes on the main points as you go through. Quiz yourself to see if you can remember all the definitions in the glossary and take note of the top tips for success in your exam.

The sound of music technology

- Introduction to the sound of music technology
- Instruments
- Effects and processors
- Recording and distribution in the 20th century.

Introduction to the sound of music technology

Sound is very difficult to describe in words. Many people have suggested that talking or writing about music is as futile as "dancing about architecture"! Where it is possible to do so, this chapter will refer to a variety of recordings in which you can hear examples of the sounds described. Over time we have developed a vocabulary to enable us to talk about sound using onomatopoeic words such as 'hiss', 'wah wah', 'whoosh' and so on, but we can also use familiar words and phrases such as 'nasal', 'cavernous', 'like a jet engine' etc. to help us relate the sound to something familiar. As such, this chapter will contain some language that is not necessarily recognised music technology terminology, but is just a convenient way of describing sound.

There are two main areas regarding the sound of music technology that we will look at in this chapter – devices that produce sound (the instruments) and devices that alter this sound in some way (the effects and processors). In addition to asking questions relating directly to these two areas, the exam for Unit 2 will require you to have a general grasp of when a recording was made; so the final section in this chapter will briefly deal with other issues regarding the limitations and idiosyncrasies of recording media through the 20th century.

Instruments

- Synthesisers and keyboards
- Samplers
- Drum machines
- Turntables
- Electric guitar.

SYNTHESISERS AND KEYBOARDS

Synthesisers (synths) and keyboards in all their wonderful variety are the cornerstone of electronic music. The development of electronic music can be traced in parallel to the development of synths, and vice versa – new ideas in music often originated in developments in technology. There is not enough space in this book to go into any detail about the history and development of synths, but it is essential to have some idea of when different instruments were invented and in common use, and to be able to recognise the sound of those which were most widely used.

The following table lists some of the most important synths and keyboards, when they were invented and some recommended recordings you can listen to so that you will be able to recognise the sound of the instrument. It is likely that you will need to be able to identify one or two of the more recognisable vintage keyboard instruments (in addition to the piano!) in your listening exam.

THEREMIN (1920)

The theremin is not a keyboard instrument, but is played by moving the hands near one or two aerials. Never particularly popular because it is so difficult to play, the **theremin** experienced something of a revival in the 1990s by people who built them for their own use. It has a very pure sound with **portamento** always appearing between notes due to the playing technique. It is often played with a very obvious vibrato.

 Theremin can be heard on any recordings by Lydia Kavina, and many sci-fi films from the 1940s and 1950s. A theremin-like instrument can be heard on The Beach Boys' 'Good Vibrations' (from 0:26).

ONDES MARTENOT (1928)

The ondes Martenot is a keyboard instrument with the ability to produce theremin-like tones by using a ribbon underneath the keyboard. When using the keyboard itself, it has a noticeable attack and an almost trumpet-like sound. It was more popular in avant-garde classical music than in pop music.

 The trumpet-like tones can be heard from 2:58 to 3:30 on Radiohead's 'How To Disappear Completely'. The 'ethereal crooning' of the ribbon controller can be heard from 0:23–1:36 on Radiohead's 'The National Anthem'.

HAMMOND B-3 ORGAN (1954)

Originally invented as a low-cost alternative to the pipe organ, the Hammond B-3 became widely used in many pop music genres from the 1960s onwards. This **tonewheel**, **drawbar** organ is often played through a rotating **Leslie speaker** – the rotation speed can be altered, giving a chorus/phasing/tremolo effect.

 The B-3 can be heard on almost any Deep Purple track, or anything by Emerson, Lake & Palmer.

RHODES PIANO (1965)

The Rhodes piano produces a sound that sounds like a cross between a bell and a vibraphone (without vibrato). It is the classic electric piano sound and can be heard on many recordings. It is often played through effects pedals to produce a variety of effects similar to that of an electric guitar. A very similar (but slightly harsher) sound is produced by its main competitor, the Wurlitzer electric piano.

Herbie Hancock uses the Rhodes in many of his recordings with Miles Davis e.g. *Bitches Brew.*

HOHNER CLAVINET (1968)

The clavinet (clav) is an amplified clavichord and became synonymous with the sound of funk.

 Stevie Wonder's 'Superstition' features multi-tracked clav parts throughout the song after the drum intro.

MINIMOOG (1969)

The Minimoog was a more portable version of the Moog **modular synth**, bringing the classic analogue synth sounds to the mainstream music industry. The cutting lead synth lines are instantly recognisable. It is a **monophonic** synth.

 Jeff Beck – 'Led Boots'. From 2:13 to the end of the track, Jan Hammer demonstrates how the cutting sound of the Minimoog, along with use of the pitch-bend wheel, allows it to compete with the lead guitar.

Walter (later Wendy) Carlos' *Switched On Bach* features the use of the original Moog modular synth (and an 8-track tape) to realise some Bach compositions.

The lead synth work by Rick Wakeman from the Yes album *Close To The Edge* is played on the Minimoog.

SEQUENTIAL CIRCUITS PROPHET-5 (1977)

A **polyphonic** analogue synth capable of playing five notes at once. It was capable of producing a range of sounds, but retains distinctly analogue characteristics.

 Paul McCartney's 'Wonderful Christmas Time' features the Prophet-5 throughout, with the opening riff making use of its polyphony.

The main riff of A-ha's 'Take On Me' is played on the Prophet-5.

ROLAND JUPITER-8 (JP-8) (1981)

An analogue synth capable of 8-note polyphony.

 Queen's 'Radio Ga Ga' features the JP-8 on the **arpeggiated** bass line after the drum intro. Also, the synth solo on 'I Want To Break Free' (2:06–2:34) is played on the JP-8.

ROLAND TB-303 (1982)

The TB-303 was originally produced for musicians to jam along to, featuring a basic sequencer. It was largely ignored on its release, but demand soared after it was embraced by the dance music fraternity. It generates a bass synth timbre with a distinctly 'squelchy' sound and is synonymous with the sound of acid house. The **resonant filter** gives the unit its distinctive sound.

 Phuture's 'Acid Trax' features the TB-303 (it fades in from approximately 1:05, then plays throughout), demonstrating the use of the filter to create sonic interest.

YAMAHA DX-7 (1983)

The DX-7 was the first commercially successful digital synth. It used FM (**frequency modulation**) synthesis to generate a wide range of timbres.

As this synth is capable of producing a wide range of timbres, it was used by many artists to emulate other instruments, such as bells, electric pianos and brass instruments. It has a distinctly electronic sound and is widely used on many 1980s recordings. Brian Eno was an avid user, making use of his programming skills to produce interesting sounds that added sonic interest to many of his productions.

KORG M1 (1988)

The introduction of the M1 was the death-knell for the DX-7 and other early digital synths, largely because of its ability to layer a wide range of sounds and its on-board sequencer. It can be heard in a vast range of late 1980s and early 1990s pop music. Most of the available sounds were much more realistic than what the DX-7 could produce because it was a sampling synthesiser. However, they still sound distinctly artificial compared to what the software instruments of today can produce.

All of the instruments listed above were invented and in common use before the 1990s. The list stops at this point because most of the sophisticated synths of the 1990s and later are capable of producing an enormous range of sounds, making it very difficult to tell one from the other unless you are a particular fan of one brand and know its sounds inside out. You would never be expected to be able to tell one modern synth from another in your examination. Hardware synths built this century will offer a variety of features: performance controls (in addition to the keys), keyboard weightings, sound sets, synthesis options, and expansion options that you would need to weigh up before buying to find the one best suited to your needs. Prior to the 1990s, you would not have had this incredible range of choice we are spoilt with today – if you wanted a particular sound, you had to buy that piece of kit!

Similarly, you will not be asked to distinguish one analogue synth from another just by listening. However, you should be able to recognise the distinctive generic analogue synth sound (or something emulating an analogue synth), both as a lead instrument and as a bass timbre.

Another relatively recent development that rather muddies the waters of identifying synths by sound alone is **virtual modelling**. Initially this technology was hardware-based: analogue synths were modelled by digital instruments such as the Access Virus, and companies such as Roland gave the user all the sounds of their analogue synths but in a digital instrument with all the associated convenience. As computers became more powerful, plug-in instruments became popular because of their ability to produce the sounds of their hardware equivalents, but without having to buy a separate box for each synth – the computer itself provides the processing power. It is now possible to buy software versions of almost any major hardware synth – especially the popular vintage synths that may be hard to get hold of in playable condition.

SAMPLERS

The technique of using everyday noises in music began in earnest with the **musique concrète** movement of 20th-century experimental music. Other composers had used recorded sound as part of live performances before, but Pierre Schaeffer and Pierre Henry took this to extremes by recording 'found sounds' – sounds of the environment around them, manipulating and combining them to create new musical textures. They, along with other experimental composers in 1950s Paris, utilised the world's first electro-acoustic studio to experiment with the building blocks of sound, and ask some important philosophical questions about how we understand the word 'music'. One of the results of their research and experimentation was the introduction of **sampling**, where recorded sounds (from any source) can be taken out of their original context and used in a new piece of music.

The tape recorder was the main 'instrument' for composers who embraced this style of music. They would use the tape recorder to capture sounds and would then manipulate them by cutting and splicing the tape, making loops (by splicing the ends of a length of tape together, forming a literal loop), reversing the playback direction, altering the speed of playback and combining/layering sounds. This process formed the basis for modern-day sampling. There were, of course, limitations to what could be done with tape; for example, it is impossible to change the speed of playback without altering the pitch.

Like many other musical inventions that have begun life in the world of art music, the idea of sampling sounds generated interest in the world of popular music. The 1960s saw the first instruments used in pop music that could play back samples (playback only – there was no facility for capturing or manipulating the sounds in any way). Of these, it was the **Mellotron** that first achieved widespread acceptance in the pop and rock fraternity. It used different banks of pre-recorded tapes (one tape strip for each key) giving several choices of sound (including strings, brass, flute and choir). It was expensive, and notoriously fragile. In the late 1970s and early 1980s, the **Synclavier** and **Fairlight CMI** incorporated digital sampling into their sonic arsenal, but were again extremely expensive. In the early-to-mid 1980s, E-MU and Akai developed samplers that were much more affordable, launching digital sampling into the mainstream.

At the end of the 1990s, computer memory and processing power had developed sufficiently to allow computers to become the perfect sampling devices. They do not have to contend with the limited memory and processing power of hardware systems, and offer greater ease of use with on-screen sample manipulation and editing. In 1997, the release of the software sampler, NemeSys **Gigasampler**, marked the beginning of the gradual decline of hardware samplers, as musicians were able to access large banks of samples and could integrate the software into their computer-based studios. However, to date, musicians still struggle with the reliability of software-based equipment when touring, so hardware still has its place in the working musician's gig bag.

The line between synths and samplers has become gradually more blurred, as many synths provide sample playback or integrate fully-fledged samplers and can use sampled waveforms as the basis of their synthesis engines.

The following are some of the more important sample playback devices and samplers.

MELLOTRON (1962)

When a key is pressed on the Mellotron, it triggers a short tape strip to start playing (max. length 8 secs). Each key has a separate strip of tape. Each pitch was originally recorded separately by live musicians. Common sounds are strings, brass, flute and choir. To change a sound the bank of tape strips needs to be physically changed.

The Beatles' 'Strawberry Fields Forever' features the Mellotron using a flute sound (which can be heard clearly in the intro).

Led Zeppelin's 'The Rain Song' features the string sound from 1:36 onwards.

SYNCLAVIER (1978)

Although first introduced in 1978, the digital sampling facility of the Synclavier evolved over the next few years.

The Synclavier can be heard on many albums of the early 1980s, but is difficult to identify aurally because, at the time, many people thought it was an instantly rewinding tape recorder. Michael Jackson's album *Thriller* made extensive use of both the synthesis and sampling functions of the unit.

FAIRLIGHT CMI (1979)

As with the Synclavier, the quality of the digital sampling evolved until the release of the series II in 1982, after which it was widely adopted by musicians and producers.

Again, the unit cannot be readily identified by listening alone because of the realism of the sample playback facility. Peter Gabriel used it extensively on the album *Peter Gabriel*.

THE SOUND OF MUSIC TECHNOLOGY

E-MU EMULATOR (1981)

The initial units of the E-MU had very limited memory and low **sample rates,** resulting in grainy, low quality samples. The Emulator II was released in 1984, bringing sampling to a much wider range of musicians due to its affordable price.

AKAI S900 (1986)

Although only capable of a **bit depth** of 12-bits, this sampler is still quite highly prized because of the lo-fi nature of its samples. The S950 and S1000 were released shortly afterwards and were adopted by artists such as Fatboy Slim and Moby.

E-MU ESI SERIES (1994)

The ESI-32 was released in 1994 and included effects such as reverb and chorus. It was adopted by bands such as Daft Punk.

NEMESYS GIGASAMPLER (1997)

One of the first software samplers, Gigasampler helped to revolutionise the world of sampling. It is only limited by the host computer's memory and processing power.

THE SOUND OF SAMPLING

When done well, it can be impossible to tell that a sound source has been sampled, just as it might be impossible to spot a well-executed edit in a multi-track recording. However, when done badly, sampling can introduce artefacts such as **clicks** when a loop's points are badly chosen. Also, any artefacts that are possible with digital recording in general are also possible with sampling, as it is essentially digital recording in miniature. For example, if the sample rate is too low, some **aliasing** will be introduced when capturing high frequencies. If the bit rate is low (8 or 12 bit), the sample can sound very **grainy** and hiss can be audible.

The best way to learn how to recognise some of these sounds is to import any sample into your favourite audio editor and manipulate it to try to reproduce the sounds described.

 Fatboy Slim – 'Praise You' (1999). This track is famous for the dodgy looping of the vowel 'oo' in the word 'should', where the loop points have been poorly chosen to create an audible step instead of a smooth, sustained note. What is less well-known is that the opening backing is a series of looped samples as well, demonstrating Fatboy Slim's true abilities in sample manipulation. If you listen carefully to the piano loop and the loop of the background spoken voice, you can hear that these are also repeating loops, but executed well. The vinyl noise is also a sample taken from the same record that provided the piano sample. Fatboy Slim deliberately introduced the sampling artefact to make an interesting, ear-catching musical feature.

DRUM MACHINES

The first machine that can claim the title of 'drum machine' was the **Rhythmicon**, invented in 1931 by Leon Theremin (the inventor of the theremin). Over the next four decades, several different units were developed, but they all had preset patterns, limiting their usefulness and popular appeal. Among the first batch of programmable drum machines was the Roland CompuRhythm CR-78, launched in 1978. It had four memory locations for storing patterns programmed by the user, but also allowed customisation of the existing preset rhythms. It used analogue synthesis to create its sounds. In 1980 Roland released the TR-808 which, although it didn't receive a great deal of attention at the time, later became extremely popular in the hip-hop scene and is still sought after today. It wasn't so popular at the time of its release because it still used analogue synthesis, so could not compete with the realism of rival digital units.

When digital sampling was first introduced, one of the main problems was the cost of memory – this is one of the factors that made the Synclavier and Fairlight CMI so expensive. At about the same time as these machines were being introduced, Roger Linn was experimenting with drum sounds using the analogue units available, but he was dissatisfied with the realism of the sounds. He realised that drum sounds are very short, therefore they should not take up too much memory, so he designed the first digital drum machine using digital samples of live drums – the LM-1. Linn later collaborated with Akai to develop the Akai MPC60, launching the highly popular MPC series.

RHYTHMICON (1931)

The first example of a 'drum machine'.

ROLAND CR-78 (1978)

One of the first programmable drum machines. It produces sounds using analogue synthesis.

 Blondie's 'Heart of Glass' features the CR-78. It can clearly be heard in the intro of the song.

LINN LM-1 (1979)

The Linn LM-1 was the first drum machine using digital sampling to produce the drum sounds.

 Prince's 'When Doves Cry' features the LM-1 throughout.

ROLAND TR-808 (1980)

Not so popular on its original release because of the more realistic drum sounds produced by the Linn LM-1, the TR-808 enjoyed a renaissance in the hip-hop scene after The Beastie Boys used it on their album *Licensed To Ill* (1986), and is still used today for its distinctly analogue sounds.

 Marvin Gaye's 'Sexual Healing' features the TR-808 throughout.

ROLAND TR-909 (1984)

The TR-909 was the successor to the TR-808, and is still popular today. It used analogue synthesis for the drums, like the TR-808, but also had digital samples for the cymbals. The TR-909 also featured MIDI, making it easier to synchronise with other devices than the TR-808.

AKAI MPC60 (1988)

A fully programmable, digital drum machine with pads to assist with programming. This unit launched the highly popular MPC series, which is still popular today, particularly in the hip-hop scene and amongst electronic music artists.

> In your examination, it will not be necessary to distinguish between the different drum machines listed above, but you should be able to identify analogue synthesised sounds as opposed to digitally sampled sounds, and should be able to spot when a rhythm track has been programmed rather than played by a live drummer.

ELECTRONIC DRUM KITS

In recent years, more and more drummers have been using electronic drum kits as they have become much more realistic and responsive. These kits feature a selection of drum pads that send a signal to a sound module containing many drum samples. They are most often rack-mounted, making them easier to transport and set up and, since the sound module provides an audio output, they are much easier to mix than a standard kit.

> Since the sounds of high-end electronic kits are almost indistinguishable from a live kit, you will never be asked to identify them in your examination.

TURNTABLES

Until 1982 and the invention of CDs, the record player (or gramophone/phonograph) was the preferred device for playback of audio. The audio was recorded as a groove in the surface of the vinyl disc (record) and played back by a needle registering the depth of the groove as the disc rotated on a turntable platter. Some audiophiles today still prefer the sound of a well-recorded vinyl record played back on a top-end record player. 'Turntable' (or 'deck') is another term used to describe the same device.

It was found that the speed at which the platter rotated could be controlled by applying pressure to the surface of the disc (slowing it down), or by forcing it to move around faster. By doing so, the playback speed of the audio would also be altered, creating interesting effects. The art of **scratching**, as it became known, has been perfected by DJs (disc jockeys) so as to make the turntable an instrument in its own right.

Turntables were developed in conjunction with specialist DJ mixers specifically for the DJ market, making it straightforward to have two (or more) turntables linked up to the mixer along with mic inputs to use for MCing. An important feature of these turntables is the ability to precisely alter the speed of rotation so that the tempo of one song can be matched with the tempo of another song – this is called **beatmatching.** The pitch of the track will be altered along with the tempo.

The technology of **turntablism** has been extended to CDs and also to the computer in software form, allowing DJs to use CDs or MP3s instead of having to stick with vinyl. Turntablists are often found in genres outside of hip-hop, such as nu-metal (for example in the bands Slipknot and Linkin Park).

 Public Enemy's 'Bring The Noise' features scratching from 0:54–0:58, 1:37–1:41 and 2:29–2:33.

ELECTRIC GUITAR

Just as synths are the cornerstone of electronic music, guitars (particularly electric guitars) are the driving force behind many musical styles including blues, rock and metal. You will not be questioned on the development of the instrument, but it is important to recognise the most common sounds an electric guitar can produce, including the most widely used guitar effects. We will look at three areas that make the most important contribution to the sound of the electric guitar:

- Construction
- Playing techniques
- Use of effects.

THE SOUND OF MUSIC TECHNOLOGY

CONSTRUCTION

BODY

Electric guitars started life as amplified acoustic guitars – they had a hollow body. When the amplification was turned up, this often led to problems with feedback. The solid-bodied guitar was introduced to combat this problem.

Much jazz music is still performed on hollow-bodied electric guitars which have a more 'hollow' sound, but blues and rock guitarists also use hollow-bodied instruments such as the Gibson ES-335 (e.g. the legendary bluesman B.B. King or Dave Grohl of the Foo Fighters).

> You will not be expected to distinguish between the sound of solid- and hollow-bodied electric guitars in your examination.

NECK

The method of connecting the neck to the body of the guitar contributes to the sound of the instrument. The two main construction techniques are:

 'Set-in' or 'glued-in' necks (e.g. the Gibson Les Paul)
 'Bolt-on' necks (e.g. the Fender Stratocaster).

Set-in necks are felt to give a darker sound and more sustain. Bolt-on necks are more convenient for repairs and modifications and contribute to a brighter tone.

> You will not be expected to distinguish between the sound of set-in and bolt-on necks in your examination.

PICKUPS

The first part of the process of amplifying the vibration of a string is to convert the vibration into an electrical signal – on the electric guitar this is accomplished by the pickups. The construction of the pickups has a major impact on the sound of the instrument. The two main types of pickup are:

■ Single-coil
■ Humbucker.

Single-coil pickups are susceptible to interference and hum, but produce a brighter, more cutting sound. Humbuckers cancel out much of the interference and hum and produce a darker, more powerful sound.

BRIDGE

The strings are connected to two fixed points on the guitar, but do not vibrate freely across their whole length – they vibrate between the nut (at the top of the neck, before the headstock) and the bridge (connected to the body of the guitar, after the pickups). The bridge can be fixed (so that it does not move) or it can be moved by applying pressure to a lever attached to the bridge, called the **tremolo arm** or **whammy bar**. Guitars with fixed bridges can be played more aggressively without affecting the pitch of the instrument. Tremolo arms allow the player to adjust the pitch of the strings, making it possible to add vibrato, 'divebomb' effects and 'screaming' harmonics.

Although you will not be directly questioned on some of these areas, you may still receive credit for displaying your knowledge in more open-ended questions. For example, if you know that a particular guitar sound is produced by a Fender Telecaster with a solid body, bolt-on neck, single-coil pickups and fixed bridge, then there is no harm in writing this as part of your response **if the information contributes to answering the question.** On the other hand, there is no point in writing completely irrelevant information if it does not directly address what the question is asking.

PLAYING TECHNIQUES

STRUMMING/PLUCKING

To cause the strings to vibrate, the player will either strum more than one string at a time or individually pluck (or pick) each string. Guitarists will use either a plectrum (flatpick), fingerpicks attached to their fingers, or the flesh of their fingers to strum or pluck the strings. Using a plectrum or fingerpicks will give the note a distinct attack, depending on the material of the pick. Using the flesh of the fingers will give a darker, less distinct sound with less HF content.

PALM-MUTING

Palm-muting involves resting the heel of the hand very gently on the strings, near the bridge, to muffle the sound a little. It is often used in the context of rhythm-guitar playing to create a 'chugging' sound.

 The intro to Queen's 'Now I'm Here' features two electric guitars played using palm-muting.

SLIDE

Slide guitar was originally developed by delta blues musicians to compensate for not having enough strings on their instruments. They used the neck of a bottle (hence the term **bottleneck** guitar) to slide up and down the strings, thus changing the pitch of the notes. Slide guitar has also been adopted by electric guitarists who prize the way a slide can play 'in-between' the frets, making it capable of producing vocal-like effects and extending the range of the guitar (a slide can be used beyond the end of the fretboard).

 Eric Clapton can be heard playing a 'wailing' slide guitar solo high in the instrument's register from 2:20–3:06 in Derek and the Dominos' 'Layla'.

LEGATO

In addition to plucking the notes with the picking hand, guitarists can sound a note using their fretting hand. This is called **legato** playing. There are several techniques that can be employed for legato playing:

- Hammer-ons: the fretting finger hits the string hard enough to produce a new note
- Pull-offs: the fretting finger plucks the string as it is taken off a fretted note
- Slide/glissando: pressure is applied to the string as the hand shifts position, sliding the note up or down the fretboard
- Tapping: the picking hand is used to execute a hammer-on. This is often combined with a fast series of hammer-ons and pull-offs in the fretting hand to execute fast runs and arpeggios.

 Almost any work by Joe Satriani features legato guitar playing in his extended solos. Eddie Van Halen is famous for the use of tapping in his playing; his instrumental track 'Eruption' features an extended tapping section from 0:57.

SHREDDING

This is the term applied to the school of very fast guitar picking. The two techniques most commonly associated with shredding are:

- Speed-picking
- Sweep-picking.

Speed-picking involves picking the string repeatedly at high speed, co-ordinated with very fast note changes in the fretting hand. Sweep-picking involves executing a strum-like movement, but muting a string as soon as the next string is plucked by releasing the pressure of the fretting finger, creating very fast arpeggio passages.

 The Swedish guitarist Yngwie Malmsteen includes these techniques in almost all his work. Bands such as DragonForce have taken shredding technique to new levels.

HARMONICS

On any string instrument, when the string is touched gently at a point that is a simple fraction of its length (a half, third or quarter etc.), a natural harmonic will be produced. Harmonics have a clear, 'bell-like' tone. **Artificial harmonics** can be produced by touching the string at a fraction of its length with the picking hand while simultaneously picking the string – this means the fretting hand is free to fret a note, giving a wider range of possible pitches than is available using natural harmonics alone. Artificial harmonics have the same 'bell-like' tone as natural harmonics, but it is difficult to completely eliminate the sound of the fretted note.

 The intro of Genesis' 'Horizons' features use of natural harmonics played on the acoustic guitar.

USE OF TREMOLO ARM

The tremolo arm/whammy bar allows a range of expressive performance techniques. At its most subtle, a vibrato effect can be created by (gently!) applying and releasing pressure at regular intervals. At its most extreme, the vibrato arm can be pressed violently toward the body of the guitar to create an abrupt drop in pitch – this is called a 'divebomb' effect. If the vibrato arm is pulled outwards, the pitch is abruptly raised – if this is done along with sounding a harmonic, a 'screaming' effect can be created.

 Divebombs can be heard in Van Halen's 'Eruption' at 0:12 and 0:39.

Joe Satriani's 'Surfing With The Alien' features the 'screaming' effect described above at 1:40.

USE OF VOLUME CONTROL

Electric guitars will often have volume and tone controls on the front of the body, allowing guitarists to manipulate these controls while playing. If a note is struck while the volume control is completely turned down, and the volume is immediately turned up, the attack of the note is lost, giving a volume-swell effect. This technique is known as **violining**. The same technique can be achieved using a volume pedal, and is commonly used in country music to simulate the sound of the pedal steel guitar.

 Mark Knopfler can be heard using this technique in his opening solo on 'Brothers in Arms' by Dire Straits (at 0:50 and 0:55) as well as at various other points through the song.

USE OF EFFECTS

Effects will be discussed more fully in the next section but, since they often form a fundamental part of a guitarist's sonic arsenal, they need to be included in this section too.

Guitar effects come in the form of **stompboxes,** which are individual effects units in the form of floor-mounted boxes, activated by stomping on a switch. Stompboxes were the original guitar effects units, but went out of favour a little in the late 1980s and early 1990s when multi-effects units became widely available. Multi-effects units combine several effects into one unit, usually providing the player with a number of floor-mounted switches to activate them, but also allowing combinations of several effects to be simultaneously activated by one switch. These provide more convenience in operation, including the ability to save settings, but stompboxes provide more routing and editing flexibility and have regained their popularity over the last decade.

DISTORTION

Distortion is the most important guitar effect. It was originally achieved by overloading the circuitry at some point in the signal chain, and sounded very harsh and unmusical, or could only be made to sound acceptable at very high volumes. Over time, the effect has been refined into several distinct 'flavours': fuzz, drive and distortion.

- **Fuzz** was made famous by Jimi Hendrix and his use of the 'Fuzz Face' pedal. Fuzz has a raw edge to it and does sound somewhat 'fuzzy'. It works much better with solo lines than with chords because simultaneously sounding notes all interfere with each other, merging in a dissonant fashion.
- **Overdrive** is the term commonly used to describe a form of distortion that is smoother than fuzz and is often used for chordal passages and riffs. It is often the 'crunch' setting on amps. Overdrive gives the guitar signal 'grit' and more 'guts'. It is often used for blues rhythm playing and, at higher gain settings, lead guitar work.
- **Distortion,** as well as being the generic term for all three effects, can be thought of as the more extreme of the three. It is used in heavy rock and metal and for much lead guitar work. It usually has a higher gain setting than overdrive, making it less suitable for full chords, but very suitable for heavy power-chord riffs. The generic 'scooped' EQ (where the bass and treble are boosted while the mids are cut) guitar sound of American metal bands is one of the more famous distorted sounds, used by bands such as Metallica and DragonForce.

WAH-WAH

This effect is commonly used in funk music and to make some guitar solos sound more interesting in a range of styles. It is an onomatopoeic name, and guitarists that use it can often be seen moving their mouths at the same time as they move their pedals!

 Probably the most famous example of the use of wah-wah can be heard in Jimi Hendrix's 'Voodoo Child (Slight Return)'. He uses the effect in conjunction with heavily muted notes at the beginning, but also with the main riff just after this.

REVERB

The type of reverb most commonly used on guitar amps is **spring reverb**. If you set an amp down too forcefully and it has a spring reverb unit, you will hear a loud 'twang' as the spring protests at your ill-handling. See page 30 for more information on reverb.

DELAY

Delay is used by guitarists to either thicken the sound in some way or to add distinct repeats.

Slapback echo is used in styles such as rock and roll to thicken the sound without causing much muddiness – this effect has a very short delay time and is almost heard as a 'flutter' immediately after the initial note is struck. Longer delays with less volume on the repeats can be used to thicken the sound of solos. This can be heard on almost any of the solo work by guitarists such as Dave Gilmour or Joe Satriani.

Setting a longer delay time that is in tempo with the song allows guitarists to create a sort of counterpoint with themselves or to set up interesting rhythms.

 Perhaps the most well known of delay users is U2's guitarist The Edge, who can be heard using delay to create interesting musical textures in many of the songs on the album *The Joshua Tree*.

MODULATION EFFECTS

 Chorus – this effect slightly detunes the signal, playing the detuned version alongside the clean signal to give the effect of more than one instrument playing at the same time. It can produce lush, 'jangling' effects, especially when applied to a clean guitar tone, or strange, 'underwater' sounds at more extreme settings.

 Chorus is used (along with delay) in the intro and first verse of Marillion's 'Sugar Mice' to warm up the clean guitar sound.

At the beginning of Camel's 'Nimrodel/The Procession/The White Rider', the guitar has a more extreme form of chorus applied, giving the 'underwater' sound.

Flanger – one of the most instantly recognisable guitar effects, flanger gives a 'swirling' or 'whooshing' effect, depending on the rate of the effect. A more extreme setting gives a 'jet plane' effect, and is used in conjunction with distorted guitar.

 Brian May uses flanger (along with overdrive) in Queen's 'Keep Yourself Alive' to give the guitar riff a little more movement and features the distinct 'whooshing' sound.

- **Phaser** – a similar effect to flanging, but it is generally subtler, providing a 'shimmering' effect to clean guitar and adding a little movement, to lightly distorted parts.

You will not be asked to distinguish phaser from flanger and chorus in your examination (because it can sound similar to either depending on the settings), but you should be able to tell the difference between flanger and chorus just by listening.

Effects and processors

- Filtering and EQ
- Dynamic processing
- Reverb and delay
- Modulation effects
- Other effects.

FILTERING AND EQ

A standard volume control will change the volume of the whole audio signal. A filter lets some of the audio signal through without changing it, but will cut or boost the signal level of a specific frequency range. Examples of filters are: low-pass (LPF), high-pass (HPF), band-pass, notch and shelving filters. Strictly speaking, a filter just takes something away from the signal but, in practical terms, most of the filters we would use for musical applications will have circuitry built in that allows us to boost elements of the signal as well.

COMMON CONTROLS ON A FILTER

Different filters will have a variety of different controls depending on what they are designed to do, but the most important controls are **cut-off frequency** (or **centre frequency** for band-pass and notch filters)**, gain, resonance** (or **Q**) and **slope**.

- The **cut-off frequency** determines which frequencies will be passed unaffected and which frequencies will be cut
- **Centre frequency** determines the point at which a band-pass or notch filter will have most effect
- The **gain** control will determine how much cut or boost is applied to the effected frequencies
- A **resonance** or **Q** control determines the bandwidth of frequencies that are affected – a high value will affect a very narrow range and (in a synthesiser filter circuit) will have the affect of audibly amplifying this frequency.
- The **slope** of the filter determines how sharply the filter will act at its cut-off frequency.

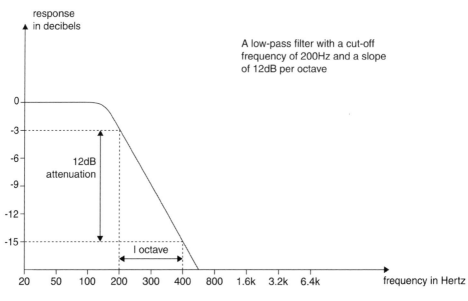

response
in decibels

A low-pass filter with a cut-off
frequency of 200Hz and a slope
of 12dB per octave

0

-3

-6   12dB
attenuation

-9

-12

-15

I octave

20   50   100   200   300   400   800   1.6k   3.2k   6.4k   frequency in Hertz

LPFs

Low-pass filters are instantly recognisable and very common. They reduce the level (lower the amplitude) of all frequencies above the cut-off frequency, but let the frequencies below this value (i.e. the low frequencies) pass by unaltered. LPFs can be heard in action in many dance tracks where the drum part begins sounding very muffled, and gradually becomes clearer and clearer as the song's intro continues. You can imitate this sound by beatboxing a drum part – start with your mouth almost closed and then gradually open it so that the sound becomes less muffled. What you are doing is gradually letting more and more high frequencies through – you are acting as a LPF with a gradually increasing cut-off frequency.

Madonna – 'The Power of Good-Bye'.

The arpeggiated synth sound in the opening has a LPF applied, initially with a relatively low cut-off frequency. It is gradually opened up just before the vocals come in.

Plastikman – 'Consume'.

This track is almost a study in the application of filtering. The staccato synth sound (becomes audible just after 2:00) has a LPF filter applied with relatively high resonance, where the cut-off frequency rises and falls gradually. The resonance value changes throughout the track, and is high enough at 8:30 to cause clipping in the signal chain. A HPF is also applied to thin out the sound, with the cut-off frequency varying as the track continues.

HPFs

A high-pass filter does the opposite job to that of a low-pass filter – it lets the frequencies above the cut-off frequency pass unaffected but cuts those below. A common use of a HPF is as a **rumble filter**, where it is set at approximately 80Hz to eliminate unwanted low-frequency sounds such as footsteps or the low frequency rumble of traffic – many mixing desks include a switch on each channel for this purpose.

 Stardust – 'The Music Sounds Better With You'.

The opening of the track sounds very thin and weedy because a HPF is cutting all the low end. There is no gradual change in this example – the filter is just turned off at 0:16, at which point the full frequency range can be heard.

BAND-PASS FILTERS

A band-pass filter is essentially a combination of a LPF and a HPF, where any frequencies outside the scope of the LPF and HPF pass unaffected. When drawn on a graph, this resembles a bell curve, where the width of the curve is determined by the Q value around the centre frequency. Band-pass filters allow the user to boost or cut the affected frequencies. A wah-wah pedal is a common example of a band-pass filter.

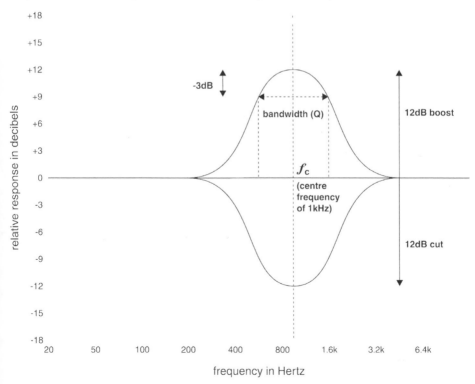

NOTCH FILTERS

A notch filter is a band-pass filter with a very high Q value (i.e. a very narrow bell curve) that is used to cut a particular frequency. It would often be used in location recording to eliminate hum at a specific frequency.

SHELVING FILTERS

These are similar to LPFs and HPFs in that they work at either end of the frequency range but, unlike LPFs and HPFs, they allow the user to cut or boost the signal beyond a specific frequency, which is then evenly applied until the end of the audio spectrum, leaving the rest of the signal unaffected. It is called a shelving filter because the graph looks a bit like a shelf. These are the tone controls most commonly used on consumer audio equipment and the treble/bass controls on guitar amplifiers.

EQUALISATION

Equalisation (or **EQ**) was originally invented to compensate for tonal inadequacies in early audio equipment. It was used exclusively to correct deficiencies in the sound, thus 'equalising' the sound. As studio equipment became more sophisticated there was no longer the same need to compensate for its inadequacies, so EQ became a more creative tool.

An EQ unit will give the user a combination of various filters that can be used in conjunction with each other. Hardware EQs are limited by the components used in the manufacture and design of the unit, including the space on the front panel for the necessary controls. Plug-in EQs as used in audio production software can offer almost limitless features and combinations of filter types.

PARAMETRIC EQ

This is an EQ circuit based on a band-pass filter, with access to all the parameters of the filter – the centre frequency, boost/cut and Q. Parametric EQ units will usually provide more than one fully adjustable filter section so that multiple frequency bands can be affected. Sweeping the centre frequency control on a parametric EQ section when the gain control is fully up or down (and a relatively low Q value) will give a similar sound to that of a wah-wah pedal – you will be able to hear the effect on the mid-range of the audio signal as you dramatically alter the frequency response of a significant chunk of the audio. Try this exercise with some songs you know really well so that you can hear what the different frequency bands really sound like. Also, try using a high Q value to see if you can tune out just one pitch in a recording.

GRAPHIC EQ

A graphic EQ is made up of a series of band-pass filter, sections with equally spaced centre frequencies organised according to musical intervals (such as an octave). The EQ will cover the full audible frequency range, so the Q value of each filter will be determined by how many filters there are on the unit. Graphic EQs are commonly used for a front of house mix to compensate for the venue's acoustics.

DYNAMIC PROCESSING

Music is made interesting by light and shade. In live music this will involve a combination of textural contrasts and changes in the dynamics of the performance. The human ear is capable of registering an enormous variation of dynamic contrasts – a range of around 120dB – from the point of inaudibility to the threshold of pain. However, problems exist when trying to capture and reproduce this full dynamic range for broadcast or distribution. The quietest sounds we can hear would be completely lost in background noise and interference, while the loudest sounds we can hear are too loud to be accurately reproduced by any analogue or 16-bit digital media. As such, there needs to be some artificial processing of the dynamic range of recorded music.

Dynamic processing is often rather difficult to hear in isolation – our ears can be more forgiving of changes in dynamics than changes in frequency – so examples of the following dynamic range processors will need to be rather extreme. By far the best way to become familiar with the sound of dynamic range processors is to experiment with them using your audio software or hardware units, adjusting the different parameters to see how they interact and change the sound of the music. Frequently compare the processed signal to the unprocessed signal to help you spot the changes in the sound.

COMPRESSION

A compressor is one of the most important and commonly used pieces of equipment in any studio. It reduces the dynamic range of music, making it more suitable for recorded media and broadcasting. The most basic way of compressing the sound is to 'ride the fader' – when the volume gets too high, reduce the level of the fader and when it gets too low, increase the fader level. This 'manual compression' was one of the ways engineers would originally have controlled the dynamic range of music. This solution is not ideal as it takes time for the hand to respond to what the ear hears, so some peaks and troughs in the volume will slip through unless the engineer anticipates the changes.

A compressor automates this process by setting a level (the **threshold**) above which the compressor acts, reducing the volume of the signal by a certain amount (the **ratio**). How quickly the compressor kicks in after the threshold has been exceeded can be adjusted using the **attack** control. How quickly the compressor stops reducing the signal level after the volume falls below the threshold can be adjusted using the **release** control. After the peaks in the dynamic range have been reduced, it is possible to boost the whole signal using the **output gain** control. This whole process 'squashes' or evens out the dynamic range of the music. When extreme compression is used, it is possible to hear this squashing effect, but subtle compression is almost inaudible and can really only be spotted by comparing the unprocessed audio to the compressed audio.

Compression circuits have a perceptible affect on the sound in addition to changing the dynamic range of the music – it is beyond the scope of this book to go into the technical detail, but you can hear a subtle change in the quality of the sound even if you can't hear the difference in the dynamics after compression is applied.

Nowadays, there is still a lot of 'riding the fader' used by engineers, but it is usually in the form of automation in audio software. The engineer can meticulously draw in changes to the volume in a graphic display that will then control the level of the track. Since it is normally possible to zoom in the display to a very high level of magnification, it is possible to have a great deal of control over the dynamic range of any performance.

Modern recordings of pop music are almost all compressed very heavily, with most recordings going through several stages of compression. This has led to the 'volume wars', where engineers strive to make their recording sound louder than other recordings. What is actually happening is that the dynamic range is being reduced to such an extent that most of the music is in the top few decibels of the available range. This can be rather fatiguing to the ear and means that musical interest needs to be generated using other production methods such as frequently varying the instrumentation, creative use of effects, filtering and so on.

Tune your radio to a station that plays the latest pop music (e.g. your local radio station or BBC Radio 1). Listen to this for a while and then immediately switch to a station that plays classical music (e.g. BBC Radio 3). You will notice that the volume dips noticeably. This is because it is much less acceptable to dramatically alter the dynamic range of classical music than it is to do so with pop or rock music. If you do this exercise in a car while on a journey, you will notice that some of the classical music becomes almost inaudible, masked by the tyre and traffic noise, but if you turn it up to compensate you will soon be reaching for the volume control again to turn down a loud section. This is not true of the pop music station which will remain at an even dynamic level – it has been much more heavily compressed than the classical music station.

This can also be heard if you create a playlist on your MP3 player that includes a mix of modern rock or pop tracks, from the 2000s, alongside music from the 1970s and 1980s. You will hear that the modern material sounds noticeably louder than the older tracks.

LIMITING

Limiters are really just compressors with extreme settings. They are normally used to prevent signals from increasing beyond a certain level, to avoid damaging equipment or increasing beyond an acceptable limit (e.g. 0dB). Limiters will have an extremely short attack and release time, and will have a ratio set as close to ∞:1 as possible (in practice this tends to be approximately 20:1). If the threshold is set too low, limiting can distort the signal because of its extreme settings – it tends only to be used to control the occasional peaks that might be missed by a compressor.

MULTI-BAND COMPRESSION

If you attempt to compress a full mix, you will find that certain instruments, particularly drums, tend to trigger the compressor more than others. This means that if there is a heavy kick drum hit, the whole mix will suddenly be compressed because the kick drum took the overall level above the threshold. When this happens there is an audible 'pumping' effect, which is usually undesirable. Multi-band compressors allow the user to compress specific parts of the frequency range without compressing the rest of the audio – this means that the kick drum can be compressed differently to the rest of the mix, avoiding the pumping effect. Beware when using multi-band processors – they can seriously damage your mix unless you know how to use them properly!

DE-ESSING

Sibilant sounds such as 'sss', 'sshh', 't', and 'ch' can be distracting in a recording. These sounds generally exist at frequencies between 5kHz–10kHz and can be controlled using multi-band compression, where the 5–10kHz range is compressed while the rest of the audio remains unaffected. There are also specialist de-esser devices and plug-ins that have a more sophisticated approach to removing sibilance.

 George Michael – 'Cowboys And Angels'.

This track has a lot of high-frequency content, deliberately emphasising the sibilance. It could probably do with a little de-essing in places (e.g. at 1:14 on 'wish').

EXPANSION AND GATING

Expanders have similar controls to those of a compressor, but they work in the opposite way – they reduce the level of signals that fall below a set threshold, thus expanding the dynamic range instead of reducing it. They are most commonly used as noise reducers, by setting the threshold for the quiet sections of the music (e.g. when a vocalist is waiting to sing between phrases) so that the background noise is reduced in level, but when the vocalist begins singing the level rises above the threshold and is unaffected.

Noise gates are extreme expanders (in the same way that limiters are extreme compressors) – they have a ratio set as close to ∞:1 as possible, thus reducing any signal to silence when it passes below the threshold. As well as their obvious use as devices to get rid of unwanted noise, noise gates can be used creatively by using them to process one signal, but **triggering** them with a different signal. A common way of doing this would be to apply a noise gate to a synth sound, but feed a drum part into the **sidechain** of the gate. The drum part is the track that triggers the gate to open, but it affects the synth sound – the synth can only be heard every time there is a drum hit. This can create some interesting rhythmic effects in a synth part. Expanders can be used in the same way so that the volume of the synth will drop a certain amount rather than being reduced to silence.

REVERB AND DELAY

Reverberation (reverb) is a naturally occurring phenomenon that gives our brains lots of information about the space we are in, even if we cannot see the space. Reverb happens when a sound reflects off its surrounding surfaces, then these reflections again reflect off the surfaces, then the process continues creating a 'wash' of overlapping echoes. These echoes briefly remain audible even after the initial sound source has been taken away. Unless the space is very large indeed, we will not hear the reflected sounds as distinct echoes. We will simply perceive a sense of space – our brains subconsciously decode the information to tell us that we are in, for example, a large, concrete room with very few furnishings, or that we are standing in a small lounge with sofas and heavy curtains. We can hear this because the reflected sounds will return to our ears after a certain length of time, will last for a certain duration and will have a different combination of frequencies to the original source sound.

Reverb has been included on recordings, by accident or design, since sound capture was invented. Unless a sound is captured in an **anechoic chamber** (a room that has been designed to absorb sound energy, allowing no audible reverberation), it will be impossible to avoid capturing some of the sound of the recording space. Close micing helps to eliminate most, but not all of the sound of the room. Ambient micing techniques deliberately make use of the sound of the recording environment by placing good quality mics, often condensers, a particular distance away from the sound source. The further the mics are from the sound source, the more reverb they will capture in proportion to direct sound. Ambient micing techniques are widely used in recording classical music, so venues with good acoustics are highly prized by classical recording engineers.

The first deliberate use of reverb in popular music recordings was a logical step onwards from the classical technique of finding the best venue – engineers would place the musician(s) in a booth, room, chamber or hall that had the reverb character they wanted to capture. This reverb sounds very natural, but cannot be removed from recordings after the initial sound capture. A room that is chosen to act as a recording room because of its acoustic properties is called a 'live room'.

Having a selection of live rooms is not within the budget of most studios and cannot be reproduced when the performers play at different venues, so it was not long before engineers sought new methods of producing artificial reverb. This was initially achieved by using either a metal plate or a spring.

PLATE REVERB

Plate reverb is achieved by feeding an audio signal through a thin metal plate that is suspended in a frame. The reverb time can be adjusted by damping the vibrations using felt pads. This method of generating reverb was commonly used through the 1960s and 1970s, and can be heard on many of the recordings of this era. Plate reverb is a rich sounding reverb with a distinct tonality, due to the sound being fed through a metallic plate. The reverb 'blooms' and is audible immediately, and has a very smooth decay. Plate reverb was most commonly used on vocals and drum sounds, and is still preferred to the digital alternatives by some engineers today.

SPRING REVERB

Hanging a large metal sheet on the wall of a studio poses certain problems. It will take up a lot of space, and needs to be kept in an acoustically treated and isolated box or it will respond to every noise made in the studio. A cheaper, more practical, but less sonically desirable alternative to plate reverb is spring reverb (sometimes called spring-line reverb).

These units operate on the same physical principles as plate reverbs, but replace the plate with a loose spring. They are still frequently used in guitar amps, as you will hear if you knock a spring reverb-equipped amp a little too hard! Spring reverb has a more metallic and less rich sound than plate reverbs. Two springs are often used together in a single unit to thicken up the sound or to give a stereo reverb.

GATED REVERB

A lot of reverb on percussion sounds can muddy a mix. It was discovered that if a reverb is fed through a noise gate the tail is abruptly cut off, tidying up the overall mix. Abruptly chopping off the reverb tail is a rather dramatic effect that became closely associated with the classic rock sound of the 1980s.

Phil Collins – 'In The Air Tonight'.

The classic example of gated reverb on a big drum sound – listen to the drum fill at 3:40. The abrupt cutting of the reverb tail can be heard on the snare through the rest of the track.

DIGITAL REVERB

With the advent of digital technology, artificial reverb became much more controllable. The first high-quality digital units were extremely expensive, but as the technology advanced and became mass-produced, compact digital units quickly replaced the plate and spring reverbs in many studios. Different spaces can be emulated by adjusting some of the important parameters of the digital reverb unit (most digital units also include presets that emulate plate and spring reverbs).

- **Pre-delay** is the time between the original sound and the first reflection. This can give the impression of room size (a longer pre-delay gives the impression of a larger room).
- **Early reflections** are the more spaced out, separated reflections of the original sound, made before the reflections have bounced off various surfaces several times and begun to blend into each other. The early reflections setting will generally determine what sort of reverb preset you are using (such as ambience, room, hall, plate).
- **Decay time** – often simply labelled 'reverb time', this control will set the time it takes for the reverb to die away. A longer decay time will give the impression of a sound being further away or in a larger space.
- **High-frequency damping** – as sound waves reflect off surfaces, they are absorbed at different rates for different frequencies. High frequencies are absorbed more quickly than low frequencies. Softer surfaces (such as curtains and soft furnishings) absorb high frequencies more quickly than harder surfaces (such as concrete), so adjusting this parameter will give an impression of the 'warmth' of a space.

Most digital reverb units will have many adjustable parameters, but we do not have space to go into them all here.

Digital reverb has been used on almost all recordings from the last three decades or so. High-quality digital reverbs are usually indistinguishable from the space or vintage unit they are emulating. Only the earliest, lower-quality digital reverbs have a specific sound of their own (they sound 'brittle' or 'grainy'). Since there are so many possible variations in the different parameters and reverb types, it is best to get an idea of what these do by experimenting on your plug-in of choice. Create a listening log and keep a separate section on reverb – the effect is so important that it is worth a lot of individual study. Try to identify the parameters listed above and the type of reverb used (hall, plate, spring or gated).

CONVOLUTION REVERB

As digital technology and signal processing have advanced, digital reverb has become much more sophisticated. It is now possible to emulate any space by sampling the reverberation characteristics and then mathematically modelling them in a reverb unit (often a plug-in). Famous cathedrals, sought-after live rooms and natural spaces such as the Grand Canyon have all been 'sampled' and modelled in convolution reverb units.

ECHO AND DELAY

All digital reverb units process many individual delays of a signal in highly complex ways, but a discrete delay unit is thought of as a separate effect in its own right. In order to artificially delay a sound (or to create an echo), it needs to be recorded in some way. Originally this was achieved by capturing the sound on magnetic tape, then by using 'bucket brigade chips' and then by capturing the sound digitally. Each type of capture gives the effect a particular sound.

ANALOGUE DELAY

The **Echoplex** was one of the first portable delay units. In particular, it caught the imagination of rock guitarists such as Brian May and Jimmy Page, allowing them to add echoes of their guitar tracks as they played. The device recorded the original sound onto magnetic tape and then played it back. The delay time could be changed by moving the position of the playback head, and the amount of echoes could be changed by feeding some of the delayed signal back into the unit again. The delayed sound lost some of the high-frequency content of the original, giving it a 'warm' sound. Many modern digital delay effects try to emulate this analogue warmth.

Later analogue delays used 'bucket brigade chips' instead of tape to store the original sound. These chips were much more convenient and reliable than tape, but were rather noisy – the longer the delay, the more noise.

When an analogue delay (or a unit emulating an analogue delay) is set with the delayed signal relatively low in the mix, it can't easily be heard as an echo – it has the effect of thickening the source sound. This effect is emphasised because of the loss of high frequencies in the repeat(s). When the feedback (number of repeats) is set very high, with a high effect level, the unit can go into self-oscillation, creating a gentle version of the sound of a helicopter taking off.

Queen – 'Brighton Rock'.

The solo uses an Echoplex to create delays, which Brian May uses to create counterpoint and harmonies. In the live version the solo goes on for a long time!

SLAP-BACK ECHO

Slap-back echo is an analogue delay of approximately 80–200ms that creates an almost percussive effect, with its close-proximity single repeat of the original signal. The repeat is generally at a fairly high level so as to be noticeable. It can be heard on many rock and roll recordings of the 1950s (particularly on the vocals and electric guitars). It also makes the effected sound a little 'thicker' than the original.

DIGITAL AND MULTI-TAP DELAY

Digital delay uses some form of memory to store the original sound (much like RAM on a computer). As with other digital effects, once the sound is in the digital domain, it is more straightforward to manipulate (using software rather than hardware), so it is easier to access more of the parameters than was possible with earlier analogue effects. One consequence of this is that the delay time can be very accurately tuned so as to be in time with the music. This can create some very interesting rhythmic effects. Many dance music artists use delay on their rhythm tracks to make them more interesting and complex. U2's guitarist The Edge uses tempo-synchronised delay a great deal in creating his guitar textures.

Multi-tap delay takes the idea of accurately timed delay a little further by allowing the user to set several different delay times in one effect (e.g. repeats at 200, 300 and 450ms) – essentially it is several delay units in one.

DOUBLING EFFECTS

Delay can be heard as a discrete echo if the delay time is set somewhere around 40–50ms or more. If it is set at about 40ms or less, it has a **doubling** effect – it thickens up the signal, sounding like two simultaneous versions of the signal.

Automatic double-tracking (ADT) makes use of this phenomenon, adding some detuning to the signals and randomising the delay time a little to create a more realistic sound.

OTHER USES OF DELAY

Delay is also used for corrective purposes in certain situations. You will not be expected to hear these examples in your exam, but it is useful to know them in case there is an open-ended question on the use of delay.

In digital recording it is often necessary to delay a signal very slightly (counted in samples rather than milliseconds) in order to play it back in phase or deliberately out of phase with another signal. This is called **sample delay**.

In large venues (such as arenas and stadiums), it is necessary to use several speaker arrays. Since it takes sound longer to travel through air than it does for the signal to travel down the lead from the amp to the speaker, it is necessary to delay the signal to the more distant speakers so that the listener hears the signal from all the speaker arrays at the same time.

MODULATION EFFECTS

Delay is also a fundamental element in several other effects, collectively known as modulation effects. When the dry signal and the delayed signal are combined and one (or both) are detuned slightly, this family of effects can be heard. They are called 'modulation effects' because they all rely to some extent on the periodic modulation of the delay time.

CHORUS

Chorus originally took its name from the way it made one voice/instrument sound like a chorus of voices/instruments. There are normally two important controls on any chorus unit – depth and rate (both controls doing exactly what you would expect). For a subtle effect, the depth control is generally set quite low. If the rate control is also quite low the effect will just give a sense of life or movement to a signal, imbuing it with a subtle detuning effect. If the rate value is high, it can create a more dramatic effect. If the depth and rate values are both set quite high, a 'bubbling', 'underwater' effect can be produced.

Chorus is often used on clean electric guitar, fretless bass and synth pad tracks.

PHASER

Phaser can be rather similar to chorus or flanger, depending on the settings. It can make a sound 'shimmer' at subtle settings – sounding a little similar to chorus, but more like a filter with an LFO applied sweeping through the frequency range, rather than like two voices/instruments playing at once.

ΓLANGER

Flanger can be described using words such as 'swirling', 'whooshing', and 'jet plane effect', depending on the strength of the effect. Some of the effected signal is fed back into the unit using the **regeneration** or **feedback** control which, when the value is fairly high, generates a sweeping, pitched sound in time with the LFO (set using the rate control). When it is applied to just the reverb or delay of an effected signal rather than the signal itself, it can produce a much more subtle, 'shimmering' effect.

VIBRATO

Other modulation effects combine the dry and effected signals to some extent, but vibrato consists only of the effected signal. It involves the modulation of the delay time by an LFO so that the pitch changes periodically, sounding very similar to the vibrato you would use when playing a string instrument or by using the modulation wheel on a synth.

 Refer to page 22 for listening examples of chorus and flanger.

Billy Joel – 'Just The Way You Are'. Phaser is applied to the Fender Rhodes sound, giving it a little more life and movement.

Seal – 'Bring It On'. Flanger has been applied to the opening vocal line.

PITCH SHIFTER AND HARMONISER

Before digital signal processing was invented, it was not possible to change the pitch of a track without also changing the playback speed. To raise the pitch of a track the tape speed had to be increased or, to lower the pitch, the tape was slowed down. It is now possible to change the pitch and speed independently of each other, without introducing unwanted distortions to the signal (if kept within reasonable limits). You will not need to know what technological magic is used to perform this miracle, but should be able to spot obvious pitch shifting in a mix. This means learning to listen out for the little anomalies that do tend to appear when pitch shifting devices are pushed beyond 'reasonable limits'. These include a part sounding a little unnatural, 'metallic' or 'grainy'. This is especially noticeable in vocal parts. When the pitch is raised or lowered by a considerable amount (perhaps an octave or more), there will almost always be noticeable **glitching**. If a vocal part has been pitch shifted up a lot, it will have a 'chipmunk' quality to the voice, as if the singer has been breathing helium.

Pitch-shifted parts are often used as harmonies along with the original. If they are shifted by a fixed interval (e.g. a perfect 5th), it is fairly obvious that the two parts are identical in every aspect except pitch. If they are shifted by a non-fixed interval (e.g. major or minor 3rds, depending on the original note), the device being used is a **harmoniser** – it has been programmed to harmonise in a certain key, so can change the interval to suit the chosen scale. Harmonisers take an almost imperceptible length of time to work out what note they are supposed to produce to harmonise the given pitch (they first have to work out the original pitch, which takes a finite amount of time), but this tiny delay (latency) can sometimes be noticeable. Also, if the tuning of the original is a little out, the harmoniser can 'wobble' between two notes as it tries to figure out what the 'correct' note is.

AUTOTUNE

Autotune is a processor that detects the pitch of an incoming signal and forces it to the nearest pitch (as determined by the user) – a bit like quantising pitch instead of rhythm. Most recent pop music contains heavily autotuned vocal parts. When a vocal has been autotuned, the vocals often have a consistency and accuracy of pitching that not even the most well-trained voice can achieve. Extreme settings can produce a very mechanical transition between notes that has become popular in recent years as a production technique.

Cher – 'Believe'.

This is the track that started off the trend for extreme autotune settings. At 0:36 the vocal steps mechanically from one note to the next. The same effect could be achieved with a vocoder.

VOCODER

Vocoders analyse an incoming signal (the modulator) and apply elements of this signal to a carrier signal. In practical use, the modulator is often the human voice and the carrier is a synth timbre. The resulting sound is a 'robotic' voice that follows whatever pitch is played on the synth – it almost sounds like the synth is talking.

Pet Shop Boys – 'Shopping'.

A vocoder is used in the chorus to double up with the lead vocal on "We're S.H.O.P.P.I.N.G., we're shopping".

RING MODULATOR

This effect is certainly not for the faint-hearted! It adds and subtracts two frequencies to produce two new frequencies, e.g. if the original frequencies are 500Hz and 200Hz, the new ones will be 700Hz (500+200) and 300Hz (500–200). Although this makes mathematical sense, it may not sound terribly musical. As such, ring modulation can be a very dissonant effect that is used to create 'ringing', 'metallic' or 'bell-like' sounds. At more subtle settings, it is difficult to distinguish a ring modulator from a simple tremolo effect.

Black Sabbath – 'Paranoid'.

The guitar solo (from 1:22–1:46) is played through a ring modulator. Listen to how the pitch of the effect sometimes follows the guitar sound and sometimes moves in the opposite direction.

PANNING

Panning is more a mixing technique than an effect. The name derives from a 'panorama' effect in cinema, but in audio it refers to the placement of sounds in the stereo field.

Auto-panning could be thought of as more of an effect – instead of placing a sound at one pan position for the whole song, auto-panning shifts the sound through the stereo field.

> In your exam there may be questions on how the instruments in a particular recording have been panned, so ensure that you have your headphones on the right way around!

Recording and distribution in the 20th century

If a question asks you when a recording was made, you should think about the following:

- The style – certain styles were popular in different eras (see the next section on 'The sound of popular music')
- The instruments used
- Any obvious studio effects (or lack thereof)
- The recording and playback technology.

The last point is perhaps less immediately obvious just from listening, but the following table will give you an idea of some of the major landmarks in the history and distribution of recorded sound.

1895	The first commercial disks (records) are produced. Wax cylinders are also in popular use as recording media
1924	The first use of electrical recording equipment to record sound – previous recordings were made by standing close to an acoustic horn (a bit like an ear trumpet, which relied on a suitably loud sound to cut a groove in a disk or cylinder)
1935	The first commercial release of the (reel to reel) tape recorder
1945	FM radio becomes gradually more popular in the post-war period as the number of radio transmitters increases
1948	Columbia Records introduce the 33 1/3 rpm long player (LP) record
1949	RCA Victor introduce the 45 rpm record
1954	The introduction of the transistor radio. Previous radios were large and cumbersome because they used vacuum tubes, but the use of transistors made the technology more portable
1956	Les Paul uses the first 8-track tape recorder to create multi-track recordings (although 4-track tape recorders were still in common use through the 1960s)
1958	The first stereo LPs are made available to the general public
1962	Philips introduce the compact cassette (mass production begins in 1964)
1968	The first 16-track tape recorder is introduced
1979	Sony introduce the Walkman portable cassette player. The first album captured using a digital recorder is released
1982	Sony and Philips introduce the CD player
1988	CD sales exceed LP sales for the first time
1992	The Moving Pictures Experts Group (MPEG) standardise the compression format to become known as MP3
2001	Apple release the iPod

The sound of popular music

The list of styles that could appear in the Music Technology AS written paper is wide and varied – anything from *Area of Study 2: Popular Music Styles since 1910* is possible. This section will lay out the main features of popular music styles, their cultural and historical background, the use of technology (though this is looked at in more detail in 'The sound of music technology' section), and will show how the styles relate to each other.

Your depth of knowledge needs to be sufficient enough to recognise how musicians have drawn from different influences to shape their own unique sound, which has to be done from a basis of understanding the significant features of all musical styles throughout the last 100 years. To help you with this, the styles presented here are organised into related sections, and each style will be covered from the perspective of:

- Style fingerprints – the musical features and uses of technology associated with the style
- Main artists and their significant recordings – sometimes this will refer to singles (shown in quotes), sometimes to albums (shown in italics)
- Influences
- Key facts about the development of the style and the artists.

Important terms are shown in bold.

All the special focus styles will be covered and clearly identified with their year of examination, and you will need to pay close attention to these as they will require a greater depth of knowledge in the exam.

Your study of these musical styles will have taken place throughout the course, and happened in many different ways. As you develop your skills in the practical tasks, you are also developing your critical and analytical listening skills – in fact, every time you listen to a piece of music you are doing this! Learning and analysing the music for your sequencing task is one substantial area of critical listening you have done, as is the similar work you have done getting to know the song in your chosen recording. The arranging task also requires you to gain an in-depth understanding of one of the set styles – you may well have studied both – and then you have to put this into practice in creating your arrangement.

There is another benefit in using this revision guide – in your Log Book that you submit with your coursework, you need to discuss the fingerprints of the style you have chosen to work in, and relate these to your own work. Use this section of the guide to help you with the terms and language linked to that style.

The route to success in the written examination is being able to put your observations into words using suitable terminology and language. Remember to use this section alongside the other parts of this guide which support you in how to organise and present your written answers.

A NOTE ON JAZZ AND BLUES QUESTIONS IN THE EXAM

You will find quite a lot of detail in the sections on jazz and blues, the main popular styles in the first half of the 20th century. It is important to have a broad understanding of the development of these styles because of how much influence they had on the later styles that emerged from the 1950s to the present day, starting with rock and roll. In the exam, there will not be more than one question on early 20th century popular music; most of the questions will be on styles from the 1950s to the present day. In planning your revision, bear in mind that you will be expected to have a more detailed knowledge of the styles that start with the rock and roll era, when the sound of popular music, and the technology, started to change rapidly.

Jazz

The term 'jazz' covers a wide range of styles that originated in the American Deep South, in cities such as New Orleans and St Louis during the late 1800s and early 1900s. As it developed throughout the 20th century it took several diverse twists, re-inventing itself along the way. Here is a short list of features shared by most jazz styles:

- Originally written and performed mainly by black Americans
- Uses **improvisation** and **soloing** featuring highly accomplished technical musicianship
- **Brass** players are often soloists – saxophone and trumpet in particular
- Other solo instruments include piano, guitar, clarinet, trombone, flute, vibraphone
- Vocals used in some styles
- Other styles mainly **instrumental**
- Use of **blue notes, modal scales, chromatic movement**
- Use of **extended chords** – 6ths, 7ths (dominant and major), 9ths, 11ths and 13ths
- Use of augmented and diminished chords; flat and sharp 5th
- **Swing** rhythms
- **Polyrhythm** and **syncopation**.

INSTRUMENTATION

- Big band, swing, New Orleans styles: large ensembles with big brass sections, drums, acoustic bass, piano, sometimes guitar and/or banjo
- Bebop, cool jazz: smaller combos of drums, usually acoustic bass, piano and one or more lead instruments – often sax or trumpet; sometimes with guitar.

NEW ORLEANS JAZZ
(ALSO CALLED DIXIELAND OR TRADITIONAL/TRAD JAZZ)

INSTRUMENTATION

Brass band or marching band instruments – trumpet, trombone, clarinet, double bass (or sometimes tuba instead), drums, guitar, banjo, piano; some vocals but mainly instrumental.

PERFORMANCE AND ARRANGEMENT

- Lively and fast
- Strong rhythmic emphasis on beats 2 and 4 (**backbeat**)
- Guitar, banjo or piano often play chords (simple four beats to a bar)
- Harmonies less complex than later jazz
- Bass often plays two beats to the bar rather than walking lines
- Not much syncopation compared to later jazz styles
- Arrangements usually based on the main melody played once through (known as the '**head**'), followed by **improvisation** over the same chord structure/rhythm section accompaniment
- **Improvisation** often features two or more lead instruments soloing together; often playing quavers in long scalic runs with few pauses
- Some use of **blue notes** and chromatic movement, but not as much as later jazz styles.

TECHNOLOGY AND PRODUCTION

- Earliest recordings of jazz made by Victor recording company in 1917 – Original Dixieland Jass Band's 'Livery Stable Blues' and 'Dixie Jass Band One Step'
- Used a **mechanical recording** process, known as **acoustic** recording
- A large horn captured the sound of the band performing
- **Poor reproduction** of frequency range and dynamics
- Victor was the earliest record company, successfully marketing **gramophone** records and the players it manufactured, signing popular classical and non-classical musicians to exclusive contracts.

MAIN ARTISTS

- Buddy Bolden: 'My Bucket's Got a Hole in It', 'Funky Butt Song' (early 1900s)
- Joe 'King' Oliver: 'Wa Wa Wa', 'Doctor Jazz' (1920s)
- Jelly Roll Morton: 'Black Bottom Stomp', 'Jelly Roll Blues' (1910s and 1920s)
- Kid Ory: 'Ory's Creole Trombone', 'Society Blues' (1922)
- Original Dixieland Jass Band: 'Livery Stable Blues', 'Tiger Rag' (1917).

INFLUENCES

- Work songs
- Marching bands/brass bands
- Ragtime
- Blues.

KEY FACTS AND TERMINOLOGY

- Popular from around the early 1900s to 1920. Enjoyed a revival in the 1950s and remains popular today
- Played in the bars and clubs of New Orleans' notorious red-light district, Storyville
- The popularity of jazz spread to other cities with black populations such as Chicago and New York, as well as the West Coast
- The recordings of early jazz artists – released as novelty records initially – were so successful that more recordings followed, and many people who had never heard jazz began listening to it
- Also popularised by **sheet music** sales
- The music was played by white musicians as well as black – Original Dixieland Jass Band for example – reflecting the cultural cross-over occurring in towns like New Orleans
- An alternative viewpoint is that the European Americans were quick to exploit the commercial potential of an African-American artform
- There was still **segregation** between black and white people in some public places, even though slavery had been abolished.

BIG BAND AND SWING

INSTRUMENTATION

- Big band: rhythm section of drums, upright (acoustic or double) bass, piano and/ or guitar, sometimes banjo
- Top-line instruments of large brass and reed section – trumpets, cornets, trombones, saxophones, clarinets
- Vocals (female and male) feature in some tunes, but mostly instrumental

> Brass and reeds together are often referred to simply as **brass** or **horns** in jazz and pop terminology.

- Jazz combo: same rhythm section as big band, but fewer top-line instruments.

PERFORMANCE AND ARRANGEMENT

- Main melody (known as the **head**) played by whole ensemble, featuring rich and sometimes complex harmony from the brass section
- **Improvised solos** over the same chord pattern

- Jazz tunes often have an **AABA structure** – also known as **32-bar** structure: four sections of eight bars, the first two A sections being similar but possibly including a varied turnaround to prepare the move to the B section; B section usually has a different chord structure
- Brass section also plays a supporting role under solos – rhythmic, syncopated stabs or harmony lines
- Piano and guitar play **syncopated chordal patterns**; may be involved in solos
- Harmony based on **extended** chords – major, minor and dominant 7ths, 9ths, 11ths, 13ths, augmented and diminished chords, use of flat and sharp 5th
- **Swing** rhythm – quavers played as a crotchet–quaver triplet pair
- **Walking bass** line – four beats to the bar, stepping up and down with a scalic movement
- Many bands played the same songs, known as **jazz standards** and written by the band leaders and songwriters from Tin Pan Alley, with their own interpretation.

TECHNOLOGY AND PRODUCTION

The 1920s and 1930s saw dramatic improvements in technology associated with music production, and the availability of recorded music for public consumption.

- Development of carbon microphones, and later **condenser** and **dynamic microphones** and **valve amplification**
- Commercial success of **gramophone** players for playback of **78rpm** records
- Development of **radio** for public broadcast
- Better microphones and amplification meant **frequency** and **dynamic response** was improving
- Quality still limited by recording medium (direct to disc) and playback system – 78rpm records and gramophone players did not reproduce a very wide frequency range
- Recording remained a capture of live performances only, though **spot mic-ing** techniques started to be used
- Skill of the musicians in producing a balanced sound was hugely important in creating clear recordings.

MAIN ARTISTS

- Duke Ellington: 'East St. Louis Toodle-o' (1927), 'Black and Tan Fantasy' (1928), 'Mood Indigo' (1931), 'Caravan' (1937), 'Satin Doll' (1953)
- Count Basie: 'One O'clock Jump' (1937), 'Jumpin' at the Woodside' (1938)
- Louis Armstrong: 'Heebie Jeebies' (1926), 'West End Blues' (1928)
- Cab Calloway: 'Minnie the Moocher' (1931), 'Reefer Man' (1933)
- Benny Goodman: 'Sometimes I'm Happy' (1935), 'Stompin' At The Savoy' (1935)
- Glenn Miller: 'In the Mood' (1940), 'Chattanooga Choo Choo' (1942)
- Coleman Hawkins: 'Body and Soul' (1939)

- Billie Holiday: 'Summertime' (1936), 'Strange Fruit' (1939), 'Fine and Mellow' (1939)
- Ella Fitzgerald: '(If You Can't Sing It) You'll Have To Swing It' (1936), 'A-Tisket, A-Tasket' (1938).

INFLUENCES

- Ragtime
- New Orleans jazz
- Blues
- Brass band
- Popular song/Tin Pan Alley
- Vaudeville (theatrical variety shows featuring music, dance, comedy).

KEY FACTS AND TERMINOLOGY

- The 1920s and 1930s were known as the jazz age, with big band and swing gaining widespread popularity in the USA and Europe during the 1930s. Big band remained a popular style through the 1940s
- The Great Depression and Prohibition in the 1920s were a time of social difficulty in the USA
- Similar financial hard times existed in Europe, with the backdrop of World War I and widespread political upheaval
- Illegal drinking clubs ('speakeasies') were popular venues for jazz bands in the 1920s
- Early record companies such as Victor and Columbia started releasing jazz recordings – initially by white bands but by the early 1920s they were recording black artists too.

LOUIS ARMSTRONG

As band-leader in his combo, the Hot Five, Armstrong was a pioneering trumpeter and cornetist, as well as singing songs and using '**scat**' – vocalised sounds similar to those of a trumpet mute, used as improvisation. He grew up around the Storyville area of New Orleans and was influenced by Joe 'King' Oliver among others.

Armstrong – known by his nickname 'Satchmo' – became a very popular recording and live artist during the 1920s and 1930s, spending time in Chicago and New York, and was also popular on radio broadcast and later television variety entertainment shows.

DUKE ELLINGTON

Duke Ellington was a band-leader, pianist and one of the most prolific songwriters of the jazz age. He studied ragtime and stride piano when he was growing up, and took music lessons in piano and theory.

He had success in Washington and New York in the early 1920s. He always called his band an orchestra, and featured large horn sections. By the end of the 1920s they had a residency at the Cotton Club in Harlem, New York, a popular venue for entertainment that also broadcast live on radio. He made many recordings and remained popular throughout the 1930s and into the 1940s, and wrote for film and the theatre.

GLENN MILLER

Miller was another band-leader who had success in the mid 1930s and 1940s in the US and the UK. He played trombone alongside many of the jazz greats like Coleman Hawkins in the 1920s. His orchestra gave a prominent role to the clarinet which helped to create a distinctive sound.

Many orchestras featuring mainly white musicians became known as '**Sweet Bands**', concentrating on melodic interpretations of jazz standards, and having a smoother delivery than the sometimes hard-hitting and aggressive approach of bands like Duke Ellington's. Singers such as Frank Sinatra and Bing Crosby would often perform vocals with Sweet Bands. Such singers were also known as **crooners**. Other artists associated with Sweet Bands were Benny Goodman and Tommy Dorsey.

Other jazz styles of the 1920s and 1930s include stride, boogie-woogie and gypsy jazz.

STRIDE PIANO

- Piano style using alternating bass notes and chords in the left hand to create the pulse, with melodic and improvisation roles in the right hand
- Blues scale used for melody and improvisation
- Often a solo performance but sometimes featuring vocals, drums and bass.

MAIN ARTISTS

- James Price Johnson: 'Carolina Shout' (1921), 'Mule Walk' (1939)
- Thomas 'Fats' Waller: 'Handful of Keys' (1929), 'Vipers Drag' (1934), 'Alligator Crawl' (1934)
- Willie 'The Lion' Smith: 'Finger Buster' (1931), 'Echoes Of Spring' (1939).

INFLUENCES

- Ragtime
- Blues.

BOOGIE-WOOGIE

- Piano with left hand playing heavily swung quaver patterns, alternating between a walking scalic pattern on the beats and octave root notes on the off-beats
- Right hand plays melodies and improvises as in stride
- Singers and other instruments more common than in stride
- Fast tempo
- Often based around the 12-bar blues.

MAIN ARTISTS

- Meade 'Lux' Lewis: 'Honky Tonk Train Blues' (1927)
- Pinetop Perkins: 'Pinetop's Boogie Woogie' (1952)

INFLUENCES

- Ragtime
- Blues.

GYPSY JAZZ

- Acoustic steel strung guitars, double bass, violin, sometimes piano, occasionally vocals
- Fast tempo; fast, frenetic soloing shared between instruments
- Rhythm section provided by guitar playing four-to-the-bar chords and walking bass or two-to-the-bar patterns
- Musicians played jazz standards as well as own compositions
- Developed in the 1930s, remained popular through the 1940s into the 1950s.

MAIN ARTISTS

- Django Reinhardt and his Quintette du Hot Club de France: 'Minor Swing' (1937), 'Nuages' (1940), 'Swing 42' (1941)
- Stephane Grappelli – violinist who played with Reinhardt on many of his recordings and live performances.

INFLUENCES

- Swing
- Music Hall/musical theatre
- Gypsy and Eastern European folk.

BEBOP

INSTRUMENTATION

Small combos; top-line instruments usually saxophone and trumpet, sometimes trombone and clarinet. Rhythm section of drums, double bass, piano, sometimes guitar. Piano and guitar also play top lines/solos. Vocals not common.

PERFORMANCE AND ARRANGEMENT

- Fast tempo
- Rhythm section uses **syncopation** extensively; driven by swing pattern on ride cymbal, but snare and bass drum do not usually play simple patterns, often adding accents in response to lead lines in a sort of question and answer
- Bass uses walking patterns but often diverts to more rhythmically complex patterns
- Very complex harmony and improvisation
- Unusual phrasing – melodic lines starting and ending in unexpected places
- **Virtuoso** performances – fast and technically difficult playing
- Common jazz chord patterns are extended with additional passing chords and substitution chords; use of **dissonance**, particularly the flat 5th
- Difficult, musician's music – hard to play and hard to listen to as casual enjoyment

TECHNOLOGY AND PRODUCTION

- Early recordings similar to other jazz recordings of the same era in the 1940s
- During the 1950s the use of **tape recorders**, improvements in **microphones** and **amplification/mixing desks**, and the introduction of **vinyl** records led to some very fine recordings of live jazz ensembles.

MAIN ARTISTS

- Coleman Hawkins: 'Picasso' (1942)
- Charlie Parker: 'Billie's Bounce' (1942), 'Ornithology' (1945), 'Yardbird Suite' (1946)
- Dizzy Gillespie: 'Salt Peanuts', 'A Night in Tunisia' (1942)
- Thelonious Monk: ''Round Midnight' (1944), 'Straight No Chaser' (1951).

INFLUENCES

- Swing
- Big band.

KEY FACTS AND TERMINOLOGY

- Developed in the 1940s; popular urban myth is that the black performers wanted a music that was their own, as swing had been widely adopted by white performers and audiences
- Interest continued through the 1950s and into the 1960s when the **hard bop** sound developed with influences from R&B; the 'beat generation' identified with the artistry and intellectual quality of bebop
- Used jazz standards with re-worked harmony, as well as original compositions
- Although acknowledged as significant in musical development and influential on many following styles, bebop didn't have widespread appeal or commercial success.

CHARLIE PARKER

Known as 'Bird', Charlie Parker was one of the most influential saxophone players. His highly complex improvisations, furiously fast yet precise, are a signature sound of the bebop style. Many of his own compositions have become part of the jazz standards repertoire, and he often performed with other excellent musicians such as Dizzie Gillespie (trumpet) and Max Roach (drums). He was at the height of his powers in the mid-1940s, and continued performing into the 1950s. He had a troubled personal life, struggling with drugs and addiction. He died in 1955.

THELONIOUS MONK

A very unusual piano player, Monk worked in Coleman Hawkins' band during the early 1940s, but wanted to establish his own compositional and performing style. His playing was fragmented, featuring pauses and bursts of intense activity, unusual scales and harmonies, and it took him a long time to gain acceptance. He was supported by his record label Blue Note, who kept faith in him despite the lack of success. He continued to write and perform throughout the 1950s and 1960s, and achieved acknowledgement as a unique and innovative musician.

COOL JAZZ

INSTRUMENTATION

- Small combos – mainly saxophone and trumpet as lead instruments; drums, double bass and piano as rhythm section. Mainly instrumental, no vocals.

PERFORMANCE AND ARRANGEMENT

- Generally slower tempo than bebop; sometimes very slow
- More spacious arrangements, still with **syncopation** but smoother and less jarring than bebop

- Complex harmonies, less dissonance than bebop
- Rhythmically complex drum parts, still driven by swung ride; complex bass lines
- Long melodic lines; improvisations featuring a lot of space
- Instrumental tones generally softer than bebop
- Arrangements also influenced by classical music, with development of themes over extended sections of the piece.

TECHNOLOGY AND PRODUCTION

- Engineers were learning to capture clear, precise recordings of individual instruments using the improved microphone and recording technology, and **close** or **spot mic** techniques. As a consequence there are some excellent recordings from the 1950s and 1960s that still act as a benchmark to recording quality to this day e.g. Miles Davis's *Kind of Blue*
- Still live ensemble performances and little use of multi-track.

MAIN ARTISTS

- Miles Davis: *Birth of the Cool* (1949), *Kind of Blue* (1959)
- Gerry Mulligan: *Mulligan Plays Mulligan* (1951)
- Dave Brubeck: 'Take Five', 'Blue Rondo à la Turk' (1959)
- Bill Evans: *New Jazz Conceptions* (1956).

INFLUENCES

- Blues
- Bebop
- Swing.

KEY FACTS AND TERMINOLOGY

- Most prominent from the late 1940s into the 1960s
- Mixture of black and white musicians, many of whom had played in the swing bands in the 1940s
- Also known as West Coast jazz, due to many musicians being based around the Los Angeles area
- Shares some of the adventurousness of bebop in melodic, harmonic and rhythmic complexity, but has more spacious arrangements and slower tempos.

MILES DAVIS

Davis was also part of the bebop movement, but became an influential band leader during the cool period. His *Birth of The Cool* recordings in 1949 and 1950 defined the style. He constantly explored new areas, going beyond cool into avant-garde jazz, and later exploring fusions with other styles such as funk and African music.

Many of Miles Davis's band members went on to have notable success of their own – pianists/keyboardists Herbie Hancock, Joe Zawinul and Bill Evans, bassist Marcus Miller, drummers Billy Cobham and Jack DeJohnette, guitarist John McLaughlin, and saxophonist Wayne Shorter.

Beyond cool in the 1960s

AVANT-GARDE AND FREE JAZZ

INSTRUMENTATION

- Typical jazz combos.

PERFORMANCE AND ARRANGEMENT

- Extensive improvisation without many constraints
- Chord structures and form, tempo, time-signature and rhythm become very loosely arranged
- Like bebop, this style was technically difficult and challenging to the listener.

MAIN ARTISTS

- Ornette Coleman: *The Shape of Jazz to Come* (1959)
- John Coltrane: *A Love Supreme* (1964)
- Charles Mingus: *Charles Mingus Presents Charles Mingus* (1960)
- Archie Shepp: *Four for Trane* (1964)
- Sun Ra: *Atlantis* (1969).

INFLUENCES

- Bebop
- Cool
- Swing.

Latin jazz

INSTRUMENTATION

Horn section, Latin percussion ensemble (congas, bongos, cowbell, various shakers and blocks, timbales), sometimes with drum kit, bass (acoustic or electric), piano, guitar, vocals (male and female) fairly common.

PERFORMANCE AND ARRANGEMENT

- Similar to swing and big band – emphasis on melody with improvised sections, large horn sections playing harmony
- Heavily featured percussion with typical **Latin** rhythms; popular dance styles like samba, salsa, bossa nova.

MAIN ARTISTS

- Joao and Astrud Gilberto: *Getz/Gilberto* (1964)
- Tito Puente: 'Oye Como Va' (1963)
- Buena Vista Social Club: *Buena Vista Social Club* (1997).

INFLUENCES

- Latin American folk and dance music
- Swing, big band, cool, bebop.

KEY FACTS AND TERMINOLOGY

- Many American jazz players collaborated with Brazilian, Cuban and other Latin American musicians – Stan Getz and Dizzy Gillespie in particular
- Remains a popular style in Latin America.

Jazz fusion

During the later part of the 1960s and into the 1970s, as pop music became more adventurous and explored new technologies, jazz musicians started to experiment in fusing new pop styles with improvisation and other techniques and approaches used in jazz. Jazz-funk and jazz-rock in particular became identifiable styles, but many other styles used influences from jazz in perhaps less obvious ways.

Blues

INSTRUMENTATION

- Early acoustic blues: vocals (predominantly male), acoustic guitar, piano, harmonica, some backing vocals
- Electric blues: vocals (usually male), electric guitar, electric or acoustic bass, drums, piano, harmonica, backing vocals
- Many ensembles were small, with either electric guitar or piano featured as the main harmony and solo instrument. Larger ensembles were sometimes used, particularly from the 1960s onwards, that might include more guitars, electric organ, brass sections or solo sax/trumpet.

PERFORMANCE AND ARRANGEMENT

- Widespread use of **12-bar** structure, though not exclusively
- Vocal style is passionate, often loud and expressive – wails and shouts
- Elaboration of simple melodies using slides, ornamentation and interjections – such as 'ooh yeah', etc. – that have become a signature of rock music
- Extensive use of soloing and **improvisation**; particularly on electric guitar and piano, but also harmonica and vocal improvisation
- **Call and response** between vocals and solo instruments is common
- Use of '**stops**' where instruments play only on beat 1, then leave space for vocals or instruments during the rest of the bar – often at the end of a 12-bar structure after a V–VI–I turnaround, or during the start of the pattern on chord I
- Use of **blues scale/blue notes** – in major keys, the 3rd of the major scale is replaced by the minor 3rd, or a slightly flattened major 3rd produced by string-bending – the major 3rd is still often used alongside this; flat 5th is often added to the scale; flat 7th replaces the 7th of the major scale
- Harmony provided by major chords with addition of 6th and 7th **extensions** – typical harmony parts on piano or guitar are based around 5th–6th–7th–6th played on crotchet (quarter-note) beats
- Harmonic lines in bass, guitar or piano often step up to chord IV and back down to chord I
- **Shuffle** rhythm – **swung** quavers (eighth notes) used in the majority of blues pieces; also emphasis on **backbeat** (beats 2 and 4)
- Bass plays **walking** lines or uses a shuffle rhythm, playing mainly on the root
- Harmonica playing is distinctive, with bent notes and **wah wah** created by cupping the hands around the instrument and fluctuating the size of the opening – much like the principle of using a trumpet mute
- Performances were often based on great showmanship.

TECHNOLOGY AND PRODUCTION

- Early 20th-century blues recordings were made in the studios that were set up mainly to record classical and jazz music. Chicago and New Orleans had several such studios, recording live performances with primitive **microphones** onto various types of **cylinders** – the **Victor** recording machine was used by many studios – and later on metal discs
- Folk music archivist Alan Lomax made many of the oldest blues recordings in the 1930s and 1940s for the Archive of American Folk Song of the Library of Congress. Many of these were done in the prisons of the American Deep South
- In the post-war era, the move over to **tape recording** and better quality **microphones** and **mixing desks** led to better recordings, but ensembles were still recorded live
- Major technological innovation occurred with the use of the electric guitar and amplification – blues players developed the sound of **overdriven** guitar, discovering the thicker tone and edge to the sound that made their music more exciting and aggressive (see page 21 for more on overdrive)

- Blues players took a lot of pride in their instrumental tone and the sound of the band, and as recording quality became better they were able to produce high-quality recordings that represented their true sound. Recordings would still be done as a live ensemble due to the interaction needed between the performers for improvisation
- Blues guitarists in the early part of the 20th century developed the **slide** or **bottleneck** technique of playing.

MAIN ARTISTS – EARLY BLUES

- Robert Johnson: 'Cross Road Blues' (1936)
- John Lee Hooker: 'Boogie Chillen'' (1948), 'Boom Boom' (1962)
- Lead Belly: 'The Titanic', 'Midnight Special', 'Cotton Fields', 'Goodnight Irene' (during the mid-to-late 1930s)
- Tampa Red: 'Black Angel Blues', 'Crying Won't Help You', 'It's Tight Like That' (mid-1930s and early 1940s)
- Big Joe Williams: 'Baby Please Don't Go' (1935)
- Bessie Smith: 'Downhearted Blues' (1923), 'St Louis Blues' (1925).

MAIN ARTISTS – ELECTRIC BLUES

- Muddy Waters: 'Rollin' Stone' (1950), 'Hoochie Coochie Man' (1954)
- Buddy Guy: A Man and the Blues (1967)
- T-Bone Walker: 'Call It Stormy Monday (But Tuesday Is Just as Bad)' (1947), 'Bobby Sox Blues' (1946)
- Howlin' Wolf: 'Smokestack Lightnin'' (1956), 'Spoonful' (1960), 'The Red Rooster' (1962)
- Elmore James: 'Dark And Dreary' (1954), 'Blues Before Sunrise' (1955)
- B.B. King: '3 O'Clock Blues' (1951), 'Every Day I Have the Blues' (1955), 'The Thrill Is Gone' (1970).

INFLUENCES

- African-American work songs
- Ragtime
- Spirituals (African-American interpretations of Christian hymns)
- European and African folk music.

KEY FACTS AND TERMINOLOGY

- Origins in late 1800s/early 1900s in the rural southern states of USA, particularly around the **Mississippi Delta**
- Played by black plantation workers and farm hands on acoustic instruments
- Acoustic blues had various names for different regional styles such as **Delta blues**, **jug bands** and **country blues**

- Migration to the cities led to the evolution of **electric blues** in the 1940s and into the 1950s – based in cities such as Chicago, New Orleans, St. Louis, Memphis; also on the West Coast in Los Angeles
- Electric blues had various styles such as **Chicago blues, jump blues, swamp blues**
- Little commercial success in the early years – early recordings in the 1920s and 1930s were classed as **race music** by the big record companies and not marketed to white audiences
- Mostly performed in bars and clubs in the cities
- Independent record companies like **Sun Records** and **Chess** emerged in the 1940s and started releasing and promoting blues music
- Independent and local radio stations also gave the music some exposure; by the 1950s blues artists were becoming more well known, though still not achieving major sales of recordings or network TV coverage
- Blues guitarists had a massive influence on the emerging **rock** sound in the 1960s – The Beatles, The Rolling Stones, Jimmy Page (Yardbirds and Led Zeppelin), Peter Green and Eric Clapton
- UK blues bands in the 1960s included Fleetwood Mac, John Mayall's Blues Breakers, Cream, The Animals
- The popularity of blues with its original audience of African-Americans declined in the 1960s as other styles emerged, but many blues performers like B.B. King and John Lee Hooker gained recognition on the world stage
- Lyrics centred on melancholy themes – relationship problems, money worries, oppression of black Americans and limited opportunities, features of everyday farming life including the weather, gambling, but also some spiritual and religious themes.

Record companies in the 1950s

The new sound and explosion of interest in popular music that emerged in the late 1950s and early 1960s was largely due to the efforts of independent record labels that sprang up in the blues era, later taking on rock and roll and soul artists to commercial success.

SUN STUDIO

Sun Studio and the associated Sun Records were set up in 1950 in Memphis, and run by Sam Phillips. As an independent record company, Sun produced music for many of the local artists including blues acts B.B. King and Howlin' Wolf. They also developed new **country** and **rock and roll** artists like Johnny Cash, Elvis Presley, Carl Perkins, Roy Orbison and Jerry Lee Lewis. These artists enjoyed commercial success with their releases on Sun in the early part of the 1950s, though this was largely regional success in the American South.

Sam Phillips is particularly associated with the use of **slap-back tape echo** as part of the rock and roll sound – this technique, along with his choice to place the singer's voice lower in the mix than other recordings, is part of what gave Sun Records its own sound. (See pages 33 and 58 for more on slap-back echo.) Having a unique sound was important to record producers like Sam Phillips, so he always encouraged singers and musicians to have some creative freedom.

Sun Records was most active in producing and releasing music during the early and mid-1950s. Many of the popular artists who were signed to Sun Records had left by the late 1950s.

CHESS RECORDS

Based in Chicago and set up by the brothers Leonard and Phil Chess at the start of the 1950s, Chess produced most of the big names in blues – including John Lee Hooker, Muddy Waters and Willie Dixon, who was also a bassist and songwriter for the label. During the 1960s they adapted to record **soul** artists such as Fontella Bass.

ATLANTIC RECORDS

Atlantic was based in New York and was well known for jazz recordings, but also recorded some blues and R&B acts, notably Ray Charles. It was an important label for soul music in the 1960s, releasing many **Stax** recordings (see page 64 for more on Stax).

It became a hugely successful label later in the 1960s, signing major acts like Led Zeppelin and Crosby, Stills & Nash.

Other styles closely related to blues from the 1940s and 1950s

RHYTHM AND BLUES

INSTRUMENTATION

Vocals (female and male), backing vocals, drums, bass, guitars, piano, horn sections quite common.

PERFORMANCE AND ARRANGEMENT

- Shares many features of blues – more focused on the vocals and melody than improvisation and guitar solos
- Generally faster than blues
- Forms a link between blues and soul – larger ensembles and more **dance-oriented** than blues.

MAIN ARTISTS

- Ray Charles: 'Mess Around' (1953), 'Hallelujah I Love Her So' (1955), 'Georgia On My Mind' (1960), 'Hit the Road Jack' (1961), 'One Mint Julep' (1961)
- Ruth Brown: '(Mama) He Treats Your Daughter Mean' (1953), 'Sweet Baby of Mine' (1956)
- The Drifters: 'Honey Love' (1954), 'There Goes My Baby' (1956), 'Save The Last Dance For Me' (1960), 'Under the Boardwalk' (1964)
- Ben E. King: 'Stand by Me' (1961)
- Sam Cooke: 'You Send Me' (1957), 'Wonderful World', 'Chain Gang' (1960), 'A Change Is Gonna Come' (1964).

Many of the blues artists and soul artists were also considered R&B artists.

INFLUENCES

- Blues
- Boogie-woogie
- Doo wop
- Gospel.

KEY FACTS AND TERMINOLOGY

- **Rhythm and blues** was a loose term used by music journalists and record companies to replace the term **'race music'** in the 1940s and 1950s – it was applied to any music by black artists
- The **R&B charts** were separate from the **mainstream charts**
- The term has never gone away, with the current usage referring to urban black music styles with influences from **soul**, **hip hop**, other electronic music and pop.

RAY CHARLES

A blind singer and piano player, Ray Charles was a pioneer in fusing different influences from **blues, gospel, country music** and **R&B** styles during the 1950s, and was responsible for laying down the early roots of **soul**. He had a lively, exuberant style, and up-tempo delivery of his music. He released many of his early hits in the 1950s while signed to Atlantic, and remained popular during the 1960s and beyond.

JUMP BLUES

INSTRUMENTATION

Large horn sections, vocals, drums, bass, piano, electric guitar.

PERFORMANCE AND ARRANGEMENT

- Popular in New York and on the West Coast in California
- Faster and livelier than blues
- Jazz influences more prominent; horns as solo instruments.

MAIN ARTISTS

- Big Joe Turner: 'Shake, Rattle and Roll' (1954)
- Louis Jordan: 'Caldonia' (1945)
- Jimmy Witherspoon: 'Ain't Nobody's Business' (1949).

INFLUENCES

- Jazz – New Orleans, swing and big band
- Blues
- Gospel.

Rock and roll (special focus style 2013)

The term 'Rock and roll' is often applied to many types of rock music. It originally applied to the style of music originating in the southern states of the USA during the 1950s. This is the definition used here and in the examination.

INSTRUMENTATION

Vocals (predominantly male), backing vocals, electric guitar, double bass or electric bass, drums, piano; less frequent use of acoustic guitar, harmonica, saxophone and other brass. Ensembles are typically small – vocals, one or two guitars, bass and drums.

PERFORMANCE AND ARRANGEMENT

- Fast tempo – 140 bpm or faster
- Energetic delivery – vocals with loud delivery, screams and shouts
- Often based on **12-bar** chord pattern
- Predominantly uses major keys but with **blues scale** for vocals and lead parts
- Strong **backbeat** on beats 2 and 4
- Often uses a **shuffle** rhythm – slightly swung quavers

- **Walking bass** line, four to the bar, often based on ascending and descending pattern of root–3rd–5th–6th–flat 7th–6th–5th–3rd
- Quite often this line is **doubled** by electric guitar
- Second guitar plays rhythmic pattern of chords – use of 6th and 7th **extensions** of chords
- Use of **'stops'** where instruments play only on beat 1 then leave space for vocals or instruments (similar to blues – see page 52)
- Use of flamboyant **guitar solos**
- **Call and response** – often between vocal and guitar or other instrument
- Backing vocals when used are mainly simple – unison is common
- **Piano**, when used, shares features of guitar work – chordal chops/vamps or triplet quavers, lively soloing, left hand playing similar lines to bass.

TECHNOLOGY AND PRODUCTION

- Live recordings **direct to tape** – any mixing was done **'on the fly'** – changing levels on the mixing desk as the recording was being performed
- Capture of instruments is often compromised by **poor frequency reproduction** due to mic positioning and spill. No multi-mic set-ups on drums used, quite often just one overhead mic
- Loud guitars and drums were creating new challenges for recording engineers – recording levels were becoming louder through the desk and onto tape, leading to altered sound through driving pre-amps hard and **tape saturation**
- Vocals were sometimes added later (**overdubbed**) to increase clarity and minimise spill
- Some early **three-track recorders** were used in the 1950s. Alternatively, overdub was achieved using two tape recorders and mixing instrumentals already recorded with the vocal recording
- Some very good recordings were achieved despite the limitations of the recording process – the microphones, desks, processing and tape recorders were capable of reproducing high-quality results comparable with more modern equipment
- The music was released on **vinyl** which had superseded 78rpm records. Vinyl had much better quality with **wider frequency reproduction** and better dynamic range
- **Slap-back delay** developed for use on vocals and guitar – single repeat, short delay time around 50–80ms, created by sending the signal from the mixing desk to a spare tape machine; the signal is delayed by the distance between the record and playback heads on the tape machine, and this is fed back into the mixing desk
- Use of **echo chambers** – most studios had this facility built in
- Sound of **electric guitar** is crucial in the music – use of **overdriven valve amplifiers** hinting at full-blown distorted sound of rock guitar that would soon become popular.

MAIN ARTISTS

- Bill Haley and his Comets: 'Rock Around The Clock' (1954), 'See You Later, Alligator' (1956)
- Little Richard: 'Tutti Frutti' (1957), 'Lucille' (1958)
- Chuck Berry: 'Maybellene' (1955), 'Roll Over Beethoven' (1956), 'Rock and Roll Music' (1957) 'Johnny B. Goode' (1958)
- Elvis Presley: 'Hound Dog' (1956), 'All Shook Up', 'Jailhouse Rock' (1957)
- Jerry Lee Lewis: 'Whole Lotta Shakin' Going On', 'Great Balls of Fire' (1957)
- Bo Diddley: 'Bo Diddley', I'm A Man' (1956), 'Diddy Wah Diddy' (1957)
- Cliff Richard: 'Move It' (1958) – generally considered the first UK rock and roll recording.

Other rock and roll artists, also known as rockabilly acts, who often blend a more country-influenced sound with straight rock and roll, include:

- Roy Orbison: 'Oh, Pretty Woman' (1964)
- Eddy Cochran: 'C'mon Everybody' (1958)
- Duane Eddy: 'Rebel Rouser' (1958)
- Carl Perkins: 'Blue Suede Shoes' (1957)
- Buddy Holly: 'That'll be the Day' (1955)
- Gene Vincent: 'Be-Bop-a-Lula' (1956)
- The Everly Brothers: 'Wake up Little Susie' (1957).

INFLUENCES

- Country
- Blues
- R&B
- Gospel.

KEY FACTS AND TERMINOLOGY

- Mainly produced during the 1950s, with widespread popularity and commercial success coming in the mid-1950s both in the USA and UK
- Developed in the urban areas of the southern states of the USA, in cities such as Memphis
- The notion of the **pop star**, with the associated fashion and ownership of the music by the young, reflected a time of change in society
- Increasing prosperity during the 1950s, increasing availability and promotion of music through radio, TV and **7" vinyl singles** all played a part in defining youth/teen culture
- **Rock and roll** was predominantly black in origin but was widely adopted by white performers; this also helped promote popularity and reflected the increasing acceptance of black people in American society

- The sound of the electric guitar with amplification became central to the music, building on the style of the **blues** artists
- Controversial performers gave the music a rebel image
- Studios/record labels – Chess Records, Sun Studios
- **Rockabilly** was the name given to **rock and roll** performed by white singers with more of a **country** influence.

Lyrics reflected the association with youth – teen life and love, getting and spending money and having a good time; also boastful lyrics talking of personal success and ability. A big difference between **blues** and **rock and roll** is the departure from the melancholy messages of **blues** lyrics to the celebratory tone of **rock and roll**.

ELVIS PRESLEY

Elvis was the first pop superstar, and is known as the King of Rock and Roll (or just The King). He had his first commercial success in the mid-1950s, after Bill Haley's 'Rock Around the Clock' had launched the rock and roll sound onto the world-wide stage. Presley's first single, released in 1956, was 'Heartbreak Hotel'. The song was a number one hit, and Presley's manager Colonel Tom Parker secured plenty of publicity for the good-looking youngster. Presley drew heavily on the style of black performers in his music. His performances were controversial – TV stations refused to show him below the waist due to his suggestive hip-wiggling dancing. He had a string of hits during the mid-1950s and into the early 1960s, and starred in a number of films which featured his music.

He had a break in his career for two years from 1958 when conscripted to military service, and though hits and films followed in the early 1960s, he did fewer live performances. He branched out into country-blues ballads and gospel-influenced songs, but his popularity had declined by the mid-1960s, though he remained in the media spotlight. He staged a couple of live televised comeback shows, in 1968 and in 1973 (from Hawaii), which was one of the first concerts to be broadcast live by satellite.

He recorded much of his music at Sun Studio (see page 54 for more information) alongside other **rock and roll** artists such as Carl Perkins, Roy Orbison and Jerry Lee Lewis.

Drug addiction and personal problems led to a decline in Presley's health and he died in 1973, aged 42.

CHUCK BERRY

Berry is acknowledged as being hugely influential in shaping the sound of **rock guitar**, and is quoted as an influence on many **rock** acts, including Jimi Hendrix and AC/DC. He learnt his trade playing with **R&B** bands, and adopted the emerging sound of **rock and roll** during the 1950s as a singer and artist in his own right. His guitar soloing and licks were energetic and skilful, fusing **R&B** and **country** with an aggressive sound. Though his popularity through singles sales declined after the early 1960s, he continues to perform live throughout the world.

INSTRUMENTATION

Vocals and backing vocals – male and female vocalists both used; drums, bass, percussion, electric guitar, piano, electric piano, electric organ, horn section (trumpet, saxes and trombone), string section. Large ensembles, including instruments such as drums and guitars being doubled up.

PERFORMANCE AND ARRANGEMENT

- Emotional vocal delivery; ranging from forceful and high energy to sad, reflective and passionate
- Shared lead vocals between different singers on some songs
- Ensemble **backing vocals** with several singers – often the billed artist was the vocal group
- **Driving rhythm** with drums and percussion giving a steady backbeat on beats 2 and 4
- Rhythmic, **riff-based bass lines**
- Rhythmic chordal parts on piano and/or guitar
- Typically brisk tempo around 120 bpm or faster; dance music
- Some slower tempo ballads
- Strong use of vocal and instrumental hooks
- Use of **call and response**
- Short songs with simple structures – verse/chorus form, often with a bridge two thirds of the way through; instrumental breaks as intros/link sections
- Melodies often use pentatonic scales with additional blue notes.

TECHNOLOGY AND PRODUCTION

- Early adoption of **multi-track tape** machines; 4-track then 8-track
- Live recording of a complete band in a single room; use of **DI** guitars and basses and **acoustic screens** to provide separation
- **Close mic** drum recording
- Vocals **overdubbed**
- High quality microphones, models still in use today as top end products
- Use of **echo chambers**
- **Plate reverb** such as EMT 140
- Classic **compressors** such as Teletronix LA2A – used on tracking and mix, though with fairly gentle settings
- Often high-quality recordings with clear vocals and full-range frequency reproduction (including deep bass)
- Stereo mixes with **extreme panning**; unconventional by today's standards e.g. all drums and bass on left, all vocals and other instruments on right
- **Electronic instruments** include Hammond organ and Fender Rhodes electric piano; very little use of sound design through synthesis or extreme guitar effects – focus instead on the natural sound of the instruments.

MAIN ARTISTS

- Sam Cooke: 'You Send Me' (1957), 'Chain Gang' (1960), 'A Change is Gonna Come' (1964)
- Wilson Pickett: 'In the Midnight Hour' (1965), 'Mustang Sally' (1966)
- Otis Redding: 'Sitting on the Dock of the Bay' (1967)
- The Temptations: 'My Girl' (1965), 'Cloud Nine' (1968), 'Papa Was a Rollin' Stone' (1972)
- Stevie Wonder: 'Uptight (Everything's Alright)' (1966), 'Yester-Me, Yester-You, Yesterday' (1968), 'Superstition' (1972)
- Al Green: 'Let's Stay Together' (1972)
- Marvin Gaye: 'How Sweet It Is (To Be Loved By You)' (1964), 'I Heard It Through the Grapevine' (1968), *What's Going On* (1971)
- The Supremes/Diana Ross: 'Where Did Our Love Go' (1964), 'Baby Love' (1964), 'Stop In The Name Of Love' (1965), 'You Can't Hurry Love' (1965)
- The Jackson 5/Michael Jackson: 'ABC' (1969), 'Never Can Say Goodbye' (1971), 'Ben' (1972)
- The Four Tops: 'I Can't Help Myself', 'Same Old Song' (1965), 'Reach Out I'll Be There', 'Standing In The Shadows Of Love' (1966)
- Sam & Dave: 'Soul Man' (1967), 'Soul Sister Brown Sugar' (1969)
- Aretha Franklin: 'Respect', '(You Make Me Feel Like) A Natural Woman' (1967), 'I Say a Little Prayer' (1968)
- James Brown: 'I Got You (I Feel Good)' (1965), 'Say It Loud I'm Black and I'm Proud' (1968).

Other soul artists include:

- Smokey Robison: 'The Tears of a Clown' (1967)
- Lionel Richie: 'Easy' (1977, with the Commodores), 'All Night Long (All Night)' (1984)
- Jackie Wilson: '(Your Love Keeps Lifting Me) Higher and Higher' (1967)
- Sly and the Family Stone: *There's a Riot Goin' On* (1971)
- The Spinners: 'It's a Shame' (1970)
- Dusty Springfield: 'Son of a Preacher Man' (1968)
- Booker T. & the M.G.'s: 'Green Onions' (1962).

INFLUENCES

- R&B
- Gospel
- Jazz singers (such as Billie Holliday and Ella Fitzgerald)
- Psychedelic rock (late 1960s).

KEY FACTS AND TERMINOLOGY

- Soul was the soundtrack of the 1960s – it started in the late 1950s and remained popular through to the mid-1970s
- It came from the large cities in the southern states of the USA – Detroit, Memphis and Philadelphia, and also from New York on the East Coast
- Mainly produced by African Americans
- Motown, Atlantic, Stax – record labels/studios
- Memphis soul, northern soul, philly soul, blue-eyed soul – different sub-genres
- Worldwide commercial success and popularity, enduring until the present day.

Many songs deal with themes of love lost or found, as well as partying and having a good time. Motown records avoided lyrics of a sexual nature due to the desire to stay non-controversial and commercial, but artists such as James Brown were not afraid to be a bit more direct.

Social issues were also avoided by Motown, despite the background of the black **civil rights movement** and the Vietnam War, which were both pressing social issues for young Americans in the late 1960s. Eventually Motown's owner Berry Gordy bowed to the wishes of some of the singers, with Edwin Starr recording 'War (What is it Good For)' and Marvin Gaye creating the album *What's Going On*, which explores social issues in several songs (including the title track).

MOTOWN

- Set up in Detroit by songwriter and producer Berry Gordy in the late 1950s
- **Independent** record company with entire process handled in-house
- **Songwriting** was done by various teams or individuals who had to write and record at least five songs a week (Lamont-Dozier-Lamont, Smokey Robinson)
- Recording of the rhythm track – instruments only – took place in three-hour time slots using the house band (The Funk Brothers) in Motown Studio A, also known as the Snakepit
- Vocals were recorded separately; many different singers and vocal groups were used, and often a decision on who was going to sing the song was not made until after the instrumental track was recorded
- Songwriters were also the producers, and once the songs were mixed they were reviewed by the **quality control teams** (equivalent to **A&R** in modern record companies) and decisions taken about which songs to release
- Artists were managed by the company; live shows and TV appearances were highly choreographed, with dance routines and costumes decided on by the label; artists were also coached on how to speak and what to say in interviews
- Motown developed some of the most successful singers of the 1960s and following decades – including Michael Jackson, Stevie Wonder and Diana Ross.

STAX

- Record label and studio responsible for the sound of Memphis soul – generally considered to be more raw and authentic than Motown
- The studio operated in a similar way with a house band – Booker T. & the M.G.'s – providing rhythm tracks for a host of singers and groups, and house writer-producers including Issac Hayes
- Not as successful commercially as Motown but still had major international hits.

ATLANTIC

- Larger record label with more links to the big US labels
- Producer Jerry Wexler worked with Aretha Franklin and Wilson Pickett, and also **blue-eyed soul** acts from the UK such as Dusty Springfield
- Close links with Stax, using their studio and band to record some of the songs, and releasing and distributing Stax's own productions.

PHILADELPHIA SOUL

- Emerged in the late 1960s; a more polished and smoother sound with big string arrangements
- Producers Gamble and Huff were behind the Philadelphia International label that produced artists such as Jackie Wilson, The O'Jays, The Spinners, The Stylistics and The Three Degrees.

JAMES BROWN, 'THE GODFATHER OF SOUL'

- Brown considered his music to be **R&B**, not **soul**, and was very influential in developing **funk**
- Raw, aggressive stripped-down sound to his songs
- Flamboyant performer and personality who ran his band with strict discipline.

1970s, 1980s AND BEYOND

- Soul became less fashionable in the early part of the 1970s, and songs that were released tended to be smooth ballads from bands such as the Commodores and singers like Barry White
- In the UK in the 1980s there was something of a revival with bands like Simply Red and Sade drawing heavily on **soul** influences
- Popular films *The Blues Brothers* and *The Commitments* used **soul** classics as the soundtrack and part of the storyline.

Country music

INSTRUMENTATION

Acoustic guitar, electric guitar, bass, drums, violin, banjo, pedal steel guitar, harmonica, keyboards, percussion; sometimes strings and horns. Vocals and backing vocals.

PERFORMANCE AND ARRANGEMENT

- The use of **acoustic instruments** is prominent – acoustic guitar playing rhythmic strumming, chops or picking
- **Finger-picking** styles of banjo and guitar are often used
- Rhythms often simple, with a strong backbeat emphasis from snare and guitar; two-to-the-bar bass lines playing root–5th figures also common
- Occasional use of $\frac{3}{4}$ or waltz time
- Songs often typical, vocal-led pop
- Close-harmony backing vocals
- Vocal techniques include yodelling and sudden switching from normal register to falsetto
- Some styles are purely acoustic, others use typical rock band instruments together with acoustic instruments.

TECHNOLOGY AND PRODUCTION

- Varies throughout different eras as production methods evolve
- The recording industry in Nashville is world-renowned – there are many top studios that have been at the forefront of music production since the 1960s. Focus is usually on creating clean, clear, accurate recordings of the actual instruments, rather than lots of production tricks. Recording of acoustic instruments is a particular skill and Nashville is noted for its ability with this
- Electric guitar sound is often clean and slightly twangy.

MAIN ARTISTS

- Jimmie Rodgers (early country): 'Blue Yodel' (1927)
- Spade Cooley (Western swing): 'Shame on You' (1945)
- Earl Scruggs (bluegrass banjo picking): 'Foggy Mountain Breakdown' (1969)
- Hank Williams: 'Hey Good Lookin'' (1951), 'Your Cheatin' Heart' (1953)
- Johnny Cash: 'Folsom Prison Blues' (1955), 'I Walk the Line' (1956), 'Ring of Fire' (1963)
- Patsy Cline: 'Crazy' (1961)
- Jim Reeves: 'He'll Have to Go' (1960), 'Distant Drums' (1966)
- Tammy Wynette: 'D-I-V-O-R-C-E' (1969), 'Stand by Your Man' (1969)
- The Charlie Daniels Band: 'The Devil Went Down to Georgia' (1979)
- Willie Nelson: 'Georgia on my Mind' (1977)
- Dolly Parton: 'Jolene' (1973), 'I will Always Love You' (1974), 'Heartbreaker' (1978)
- Shania Twain: Come on Over (1997).

INFLUENCES

- European folk music (especially British and Irish)
- Blues
- Many influences and fusions with other contemporary styles throughout the 20th century.

KEY FACTS AND TERMINOLOGY

- Country music started in the early 20th century in the southern states of the USA. It was generally played by European-origin settlers
- Associated with cowboys in the early years, truck drivers in more recent times
- Lyrics often refer to the rural country lifestyle in the southern states and the American West
- Many sub-genres such as bluegrass – fast, entirely acoustic music, often instrumental, featuring banjo and violin; Western swing – taking influence from the popular swing bands in the 1930s and 1940s to play jazz-influenced songs
- The recording industry in Nashville is one of the biggest centres anywhere in the world. Many rock bands have recorded there, including The Rolling Stones
- Has huge worldwide following and sales despite not having much chart success.

Rock and pop in the 1960s

After the explosion of youth culture and interest in music that accompanied **rock and roll** in the 1950s, young bands started forming throughout the USA and in Britain. Influences came from the American sounds of **rock and roll**, **R&B** and early **soul** and **Motown**, but the music quickly evolved in different directions, giving the decade a rich musical heritage.

New musical styles that emerged were broadly classed as **rock**, and there are various sub-genres within this. Particularly in Britain, songs with strong melody, harmony and more complex forms and arrangements than **rock and roll** or **R&B** were typical (The Beatles, The Animals, The Hollies, The Zombies). In the US a strong **folk-rock** or **country-rock** tradition took shape (Bob Dylan, Neil Young, The Beach Boys, Janis Joplin, Joni Mitchell). Bands with a harder edge to their sound also emerged, such as The Rolling Stones, The Kinks and The Who. These bands influenced the development of **heavy metal** in the 1970s. Later in the decade **psychedelic rock** bands emerged such as Pink Floyd and The Small Faces. These bands had a big influence on the **progressive rock** of the 1970s.

It's hard to categorise a lot of the groups in this era, since they made use of so many influences – blues, R&B, gospel, soul, country, folk, rock and roll, and even classical music. Many groups also experimented with different styles at various stages of their career, or regularly mixed up soft ballads with harder, R&B-influenced music.

UK Rock and pop in the 1960s

THE BEATLES

Probably the single most influential band in the story of popular music, their development is closely linked to the changes in music in the 1960s.

INSTRUMENTATION

Vocals (lead shared by John Lennon and Paul McCartney; George Harrison and Ringo Starr also sang lead on some songs), backing vocals from all band members, drums, bass, electric guitar, acoustic guitar, 12-string acoustic guitar, piano, percussion; ensembles became more diverse to include orchestral sections, electronic keyboards and experimental studio sounds.

PERFORMANCE AND ARRANGEMENT

- Early songs were based on **rock and roll**, **R&B** and **Motown/soul** sounds
- Energetic, bright and lively; often quite melodic and sweet but sometimes more gritty and rocky (particularly with Lennon singing)
- Later works had diverse instrumentation, complex structures, changing time signatures and keys
- Use of **sonic experimentation** – recording ambient sound to mix with the music, reverse tape recordings, use of extreme reverb and delay settings, effects such as phasing and flange.

ALBUMS BY THE BEATLES

PLEASE PLEASE ME (1963)

- The success of the first two Beatles singles 'Love me Do' and 'Please Please Me' – both Lennon-McCartney compositions – and their growing reputation as a live act, led record company EMI to rush the release of their first album *Please Please Me*
- More-or-less captured as live performances of their live set, recorded to **two-track** tape with instruments on one track and vocals on the other, then mixed to **mono**
- Stayed at number one in the album chart for 30 weeks
- The sound was heavily influenced by R&B and American popular sound; lively guitar-led, catchy melodic pop
- Also included 'I Saw Her Standing There' and several covers, including the R&B classic 'Twist and Shout'.

WITH THE BEATLES (1963)

- Included the singles 'She Loves You' and 'I Want to Hold Your Hand', and showed increasing sophistication in the writing and performing. Both singles were massively popular, selling over a million copies each in the UK, and the album also sold over a million copies, knocking their previous album off the number one spot.
- The sound was still straight-up rock/pop, but with some more diverse instrumentation that included a range of percussion, Hammond organ and harmonica. Mainly Lennon-McCartney compositions, but also again included more R&B covers such as 'Roll Over Beethoven' and 'Money (That's What I Want)'.
- There was use of **sound-on-sound overdub** (adding extra tracks to pre-mixed recording using two tape machines), which included some **double-tracked** vocals. The album was released in **mono** and **stereo** versions. The early use of stereo included decisions we would find strange today, such as all the drums and bass on one side, guitars and vocals on the other side, and little panned centrally, leaving a 'hole' in the middle of the image.
- The album marked the start of Beatlemania in the UK, with hysterically screaming crowds greeting them at gigs and other TV and public appearances. Similar scenes followed in 1964 when they toured America, and marked the start of the **British Invasion**. In April 1964, The Beatles had the top five singles in the US charts and the top two albums.

A HARD DAY'S NIGHT (1964)

- The soundtrack for the film of the same name, starring The Beatles as youthful, energetic and somewhat chaotic figures. The title track and 'Can't Buy Me Love' were successful singles. The album also featured some instrumentals and folk-influenced songs, featuring George Harrison's acoustic guitar.
- Recorded onto four track multi-track and mixed in both **mono** and **stereo** versions.

BEATLES FOR SALE (1964)

- Recording was squeezed in between heavy touring demands. This album had some dark and melancholy songs on it such as 'No Reply', 'I'm a Loser' and 'Baby's in Black'. 'Eight Days a Week' was recorded in several different takes, points to **early studio experimentation** and includes a **fade in** at the start. No singles came off the album, though 'I Feel Fine' was recorded in the same sessions.

HELP! (1965)

- This album made use of the expanding capability of recording techniques by including more **overdubs**, and orchestral instruments are featured in 'Yesterday', and 'You've Got to Hide Your Love Away'. The title track, 'Yesterday' and 'Ticket to Ride' were notable singles, and this album again was accompanied by a film of the same name.

RUBBER SOUL (1965)

▪ Like all the previous albums, this was also recorded in a short space of time. But it managed to combine some more diverse and unusual approaches, including the use of sitar on 'Norwegian Wood', folk influences on that song and others, and heavy treatments of piano including **sped-up recordings** and heavy **compression**. Producer George Martin takes a lot of credit for his production work with The Beatles.

REVOLVER (1966)

▪ This album was made in more relaxed circumstances as The Beatles took a break from touring and recording beforehand. Though more rocky than *Rubber Soul*, it continued the experimentation with **classical** elements, notably on 'Eleanor Rigby' with the stark string arrangement. The **psychedelic** influence also started to emerge, with 'Tomorrow Never Knows' featuring **tape loops**, **vocal effects** and **reverse guitar**. This was also the first album to use **automatic double tracking**. Songs were starting to explore political and social themes.

SGT. PEPPER'S LONELY HEARTS CLUB BAND (1967)

▪ Widely acclaimed as one of the finest albums ever released in terms of songwriting, performances, recording quality and adventurous production. A lot of the songs used a story-based narrative, touching on a wide range of themes and views on life. Overdubbing was used widely, as were more experiments with varied tape speed playback, playing vocals and guitars through a **Leslie speaker**, effects like **flanging**, **wah-wah** and **fuzz** and the use of a new keyboard instrument, the **Mellotron**.

▪ Tracks like 'Lucy In the Sky With Diamonds' and 'A Day In the Life' are full or these radical approaches.

MAGICAL MYSTERY TOUR (1967)

▪ The music from the film of the same name was released as an extended play 6-track set. The songs continued the psychedelic sound of *Sgt. Pepper's*, with 'I Am the Walrus' being a good example of experimentation, with its effects and sound collages. The film itself was badly received; directed by The Beatles themselves, it was seen as disjointed and self-indulgent by the media, and for the first time the band received criticism of their work in the press.

THE BEATLES (ALSO KNOWN AS THE WHITE ALBUM) (1968)

▪ A double album that continued the psychedelic themes of *Sgt. Pepper's Lonely Hearts Club Band*, with a wide range of styles from typical rock/pop to acoustic offerings and music-hall influences. It was during this time that tensions started to create problems between the members of the band. The album was their first to be recorded on **8-track**, and produced many notable songs such as 'Dear Prudence', 'Let It Be', 'Blackbird' and 'While My Guitar Gently Weeps' (featuring Eric Clapton).

YELLOW SUBMARINE (1969)

- This was another film soundtrack for the animated film of the same title. Quite a few of the songs were re-worked from earlier versions, and the second side was an orchestral score composed by The Beatles' producer George Martin.

ABBEY ROAD (1969)

- This was the last album The Beatles recorded together before the band split. Features several hits including 'Something', 'Come Together' and 'Here Comes The Sun'. Named after the studio where The Beatles recorded most of their work, belonging to record company EMI. This was recorded on 8-track and made use of the **Moog synthesiser**. Generally regarded as another excellent example of fine recording, songwriting and production.

LET IT BE (1970)

- The recording sessions for this album were actually completed before *Abbey Road*, and the release came after The Beatles had split up. Generally seen as the weakest of their albums, there are strong offerings in the title track as well as 'The Long and Winding Road' and 'Get Back'.

KEY FACTS AND TERMINOLOGY

- Formed in their home town of Liverpool in the early 1960s, and went to play and live in Germany for a time before being signed to EMI on the back of widespread live success
- First band to achieve worldwide recognition
- Huge international sales of all their work continue today
- Early sound was known as **Merseybeat**
- More diverse, later sound had strong elements of psychedelic rock
- They had stopped performing live by the time of *Sgt. Pepper's Lonely Hearts Club Band*
- Like rock and roll in the USA, the bands of the 1960s had a rebel image that included personal freedom, sexual expression, taking drugs and anti-establishment political declarations.

SOLO CAREERS AFTER THE BEATLES

John Lennon moved to America and produced music exploring spiritual and political issues, with songs like 'Imagine' and 'Instant Karma'. His success was mixed, although the *Imagine* album was very popular, and by the mid-1970s he had stopped making music. He was shot dead in New York in 1980.

Paul McCartney's band Wings was a popular outfit in the 1970s, particularly with their album *Band On The Run*. He later continued as a solo artist and still makes high profile appearances.

George Harrison explored folk and Indian-influenced styles, 'My Sweet Lord' bringing a big hit, but did not sustain a long career.

Ringo Starr released a number of solo albums. The first was *Sentimental Journey*, with arrangements by Quincy Jones, and this was followed by the country-influenced *Beaucoups of Blues*, which was fairly successful in the US and UK. He played drums on some George Harrison and John Lennon solo projects during the 70s, and continues to record and perform live until the current day.

THE ROLLING STONES

INSTRUMENTATION

Vocals, backing vocals, electric guitar, bass, drums, percussion; piano/keyboards, strings and horns on occasion.

PERFORMANCE AND ARRANGEMENT

- Heavily influenced by Chicago blues and Chuck Berry's **rock and roll** guitar
- Mick Jagger's raunchy vocals and Keith Richard's blues-rock guitar give them an edgy, gritty and hard sound
- Generally stick to simple verse–chorus–bridge–solo song structures, though have produced some more adventurous and experimental work at times.

KEY FACTS AND TERMINOLOGY

- Rivals to The Beatles for popularity in the mid to late 1960s
- Part of the **British Invasion** that enjoyed popularity in the USA in the mid to late 1960s
- Continued to write, record and perform successfully throughout the 1970s and 1980s and remain active today.

RECORDINGS

The Rolling Stones have released a huge number of albums, sometimes several in a year. Many have been successful in reaching number one or getting close, and many highly acknowledged releases came in the late 1960s, throughout the 1970s and into the 1980s: *Their Satanic Majesties Request* (1967), *Beggars Banquet* (1968), *Let It Bleed* (1969), *Sticky Fingers* (1971), *Exile on Main Street* (1972), *Goat's Head Soup* (1973), *It's Only Rock 'n' Roll* (1974), *Black and Blue* (1976), *Some Girls* (1978), *Emotional Rescue* (1980), *Tattoo You* (1981).

Successful singles include:

- 1964: 'It's All Over Now', 'Time Is On My Side', 'Little Red Rooster'
- 1965: 'The Last Time', '(I Can't Get No) Satisfaction', 'Get Off My Cloud'

- 1966: 'Lady Jane'
- 1967: 'Let's Spend The Night Together', 'Ruby Tuesday'
- 1968: 'Jumpin' Jack Flash'
- 1969: 'Honky Tonk Woman'
- 1971: 'Brown Sugar', 'Wild Horses'
- 1973: 'Angie'
- 1978: 'Miss You'

Most of these are hard, **bluesy rock**, but a few show The Stones' ability with softer ballads, using country and other influences – notably 'Ruby Tuesday', 'Angie' and the disco-influenced 'Miss You'.

THE WHO

INSTRUMENTATION

Vocals, backing vocals, guitar, bass, drums, percussion; synthesiser and keyboards, horns.

PERFORMANCE AND ARRANGEMENT

- Extremely high energy and aggressive performers; smashed up guitars and drum kits as part of their act
- Many songs were hard, driving rock with melodic bass lines; also wrote songs with complex instrumentation and structures
- Guitarist Pete Townshend used the term **power pop** to describe their more mainstream music.

KEY FACTS AND TERMINOLOGY

- Associated with **mod** culture – youth sub-culture who wore sharp suits and rode scooters
- Guitarist Pete Townshend known for '**windmill**' guitar playing style
- Developed **rock opera** with their albums *Tommy* and *Quadrophenia*
- Used **synthesisers** extensively in the early 1970s
- Started the fashion for dressing in clothes made from Union Jacks, adopted by the mods.

RECORDINGS

Early single successes with 'My Generation', 'Substitute' and 'I Can See for Miles' in the mid-1960s; their first three albums were *My Generation, A Quick One* and *The Who Sell Out*. In 1969 the album *Tommy* was the first **rock opera**, telling the story of a deaf, dumb and blind boy. The song 'Pinball Wizard' from the double album is another classic Who track.

In 1971 they released their next album *Who's Next*, which used **synthesisers** for **drones** and **sound effects**, and experimental approaches to sound including Townshend's use of an **envelope follower** on his guitar. The album also used complex structures that were more **prog rock** than the earlier hard rock style.

Quadrophenia, released in 1973, was a second rock opera, and included themes for each of the band members, also designed to represent four different aspects of the main character's 'quadrophenic' personality. *Quadrophenia* was made into a film in 1979.

Several more albums followed in the 1970s, which were successful but not to the degree of their earlier work. When drummer Keith Moon died of a drug overdose in 1978, and coupled with the birth of **punk**, the band struggled to stay together and find interest in their music, and eventually drifted apart. They reformed the band on several occasions, with mixed success, though in the 1990s their concerts met with acclaim.

OTHER BRITISH BANDS TO EMERGE IN THE 1960s

THE KINKS

- A mix of hard rock, folk and musical theatre influences
- The line-up consisted of electric and acoustic guitar, plus drums and bass
- 'You Really Got Me' is one of the most distinctive rock songs of the decade, and 'Waterloo Sunset' is also a classic rock track.

THE SMALL FACES

- Vocals – by the heavily soul-influenced Steve Marriot – guitar, drums, bass and keyboards, making use of electric piano and electric organ
- Like The Who they were seen as a **mod** band with strong influences from R&B and soul, but became more recognised as a psychedelic band, with 'Itchycoo Park' (1967) using **flanging** – probably the first released example of this technique – and surreal lyrical imagery to create a mind-bending delivery
- In 1968 they released the **concept album** *Ogden's Nut Gone Flake,* based on a fairy tale-like story of Happiness Stan, with narration in between tracks and songs to tell the story. The highly popular song 'Lazy Sunday Afternoon' was from this album. They had split up by the end of the 1960s with the members going on to work in different bands.

THE ANIMALS

- Vocals, guitar, bass, drums and keyboards
- Heavily influenced by **blues**, but also taking ideas from **folk** and **R&B**
- Big international hit in 1964 with 'House of the Rising Sun', followed by 'We Gotta Get Out of this Place' (1965).

THE HOLLIES

- Vocals, backing vocals which were a big feature, guitar, drums, bass, keyboards
- **R&B**, **soul** and **folk**-influenced sound; vocal harmonies featured prominently
- Enjoyed success in the USA but were one of the last **British Invasion** bands
- 'He Ain't Heavy, He's My Brother' (1969) is their best known song; also known for 'The Air that I Breathe' (1974).

THE SPENCER DAVIS GROUP

- Also had strong **soul** and **R&B** influences, with prominence given to Steve Winwood's **Hammond organ** playing
- Popular in the mid-1960s, they are best known for 'Keep On Running' and 'Gimme Some Lovin''.

THE YARDBIRDS

- Known as a British blues band initially, the guitar-driven band had three guitar greats in the line-up at different times – Eric Clapton, Jeff Beck and Jimmy Page, who all went on to notable success elsewhere
- The early 1960s line-up with Clapton was bluesy; Beck changed the sound with heavy, distorted guitar tones, and the use of **feedback**. Jimmy Page took over in the late 1960s and experimented with playing guitar with a violin bow and use of **wah wah**.

THE MOODY BLUES

- Started out as an **R&B** band in the mid-1960s, but developed a rich, lush sound that combined rock guitars with big vocal harmonies, high-pitched lead vocal and keyboards and strings. They are most associated with the **psychedelic rock** and early **progressive rock** styles.

MAINSTREAM POP IN BRITAIN DURING THE 1960s

While some of the pioneering and ground-breaking bands had success in terms of sales and critical acclaim, there were a lot of other bands and artists who were popular without being at the cutting-edge: Cliff Richard and The Shadows, Sandie Shaw, Cilla Black, Lulu and The Dave Clark Five.

American rock and pop in the 1960s

The American music charts were dominated by the success of the **British Invasion** in the early 1960s, as well as the **soul** sounds emerging from the southern United States. Rock and roll had lost its popularity, and America was looking for its own new sound. What emerged was the **folk-rock** and **country-rock** styles, and also harder **blues rock** influences. Towards the end of the decade the **psychedelic rock** sound was also adopted in the USA.

BOB DYLAN

INSTRUMENTATION

Solo – acoustic guitar, vocals and harmonica; later with rock band line-up.

PERFORMANCE AND ARRANGEMENT

- Folk-influenced composition; songs with simple chordal accompaniment but clever use of melody and chord structures
- Vocal tone that many find unpleasant; quite nasal and whiny
- Poetic lyrics exploring politics and philosophy – message music.

KEY FACTS AND TERMINOLOGY

- 1963 single 'Blowin' in the Wind' was one of his early successes, together with the album *The Freewheelin' Bob Dylan* released at the same time.
- Dylan's songwriting skill was being noticed by other bands, with several songs recorded by different artists like The Byrds and The Hollies.
- He was closely involved with the American **civil rights movement**, campaigning for equality through marches and demonstrations, and later in the decade against the Vietnam war.
- His third album from 1964, *The Times They Are a-Changin'*, contained political songs about the issues of poverty, racism and the need for social change. The title track is one of Dylan's best known songs.
- The influence of The Beatles and other rock acts led to the inclusion of electric guitars and a rock band line-up for Dylan's 1965 album *Bringin' It All Back Home*. Half of the songs were done with the rock band and half were acoustic. Several great Dylan songs were on this record – 'Hey Mr Tambourine Man', 'Maggie's Farm', 'Subterranean Homesick Blues', 'It's Alright Ma (I'm Only Bleeding)' and 'It's All Over Now Baby Blue'.
- The next albums in 1965 and 1966 – *Highway 61 Revisited* and *Blonde on Blonde* – continued the electric country-rock line-up, and brought another hit – 'Like a Rolling Stone'.
- Further hit songs followed later in the 1960s including 'Lay Lady Lay' and 'Knockin' On Heaven's Door'.
- Dylan continued to write and perform with a wide range of artists during the 1970s, having established himself as one of the top songwriters in rock and pop music, and remains active today – on the road with 'the Never Ending Tour'.

Other important folk-rock and country-rock artists include Neil Young, Crosby, Stills & Nash, Joni Mitchell, The Allman Brothers, and The Eagles (who wrote 'Hotel California').

OTHER 1960s STYLES AND THE SOUND OF THE 1970s

The creativity of 1960s rock and pop music laid the foundation for many styles that would emerge in the next 50 years up to the present day. The 1970s continued to forge new sounds and styles, some due to the inventiveness of the musicians, bands and songwriters, and some due to the advances in technology and new ways of working with it.

During the 1970s America would produce the styles of **funk**, **disco**, country-influenced **soft rock**, and **hip hop** at the end of the decade; in the UK the sound of **heavy rock**, **progressive rock** and **glam** was followed by **punk** and **new wave**. At the same time the sounds of **reggae** from Jamaica became influential in the popular-music world.

This short summary is given here because many of the styles that followed during the 1980s, 1990s and into the 2000s have their origins very much in bands of the 1960s and 1970s. The technology changed the sound, through increasingly **sophisticated production methods** in the 1980s and beyond, and naturally the artists and studios continually attempt to develop new approaches, but much of the popular music of the last 30 years can be seen to take its influence from earlier styles.

Psychedelic rock

INSTRUMENTATION

Classic rock band line-up with guitars, drums, bass and often keyboards; vocals and backing vocals; unusual instruments such as sitar, mandolin, dulcimer and the **Mellotron** keyboard, an early sampler.

PERFORMANCE AND ARRANGEMENT

- **Guitars** are used prominently, both as rhythm and solo instruments
- **Unusual timbres** and open, 'spacey' textures
- Songs could often have quite loose forms, with extended **jamming** and soloing over grooves and chord patterns
- Vocals also given a spacey quality – dreamy, sparse and slow moving
- **Tempo, key** and **time signature** changes used to provide shifts in mood
- Songs could be long and complex.

TECHNOLOGY AND PRODUCTION

- Guitar sounds use plenty of **processing** – distortion, feedback, fuzz, phaser, echo/delay, Leslie speaker
- **Mellotron sampler** keyboard used to produce unusual timbres – choir, flute, strings. Often used for pads or drones

- Large amounts of **reverb** and **delay** used to produce unreal-sounding textures. Could be used on any part of the mix such as vocals, guitars, keyboards, or solo instruments like flute
- Phasers and flangers popular as well for similar reasons
- **Synthesisers** used for capability to produce unusual sounds
- **Tape loops** and **ambient recordings** used to add strange non-musical sounds and textures.

MAIN ARTISTS

- Grateful Dead: *The Grateful Dead* (1967)
- Country Joe and the Fish: *Electric Music for the Mind and Body* (1967)
- The Doors: *The Doors* (1967)
- Frank Zappa: *Freak Out* (1966)
- Captain Beefheart: *Trout Mask Replica* (1969)
- Tangerine Dream: *Electronic Meditation* (1970)
- Hawkwind: *Hawkwind* (1970), 'Silver Machine' (1972)
- Gong: *Flying Teapot* (1973).

Many bands had periods or just some songs where the psychedelic influence was evident:

- The Beatles: 'Day Tripper' (1965), 'Lucy In the Sky With Diamonds', 'I Am The Walrus' (1967)
- The Who: 'I Can See for Miles' (1967)
- The Rolling Stones: 'Paint It, Black' (1966)
- The Small Faces: *Ogden's Nut Gone Flake* (1968)
- Pink Floyd: early albums, listed under the progressive rock section (page 79)
- Jimi Hendrix: see heavy rock section (page 81) for information about recordings.

INFLUENCES

- UK rock
- Folk rock
- Experimental music such as musique concrète.

KEY FACTS AND TERMINOLOGY

- Occurred mainly in the later part of the 1960s and early 1970s. Linked to the **beat generation** culture based around Los Angeles and San Francisco, and the free festivals like Woodstock in the USA and the Isle of Wight festival in the UK
- The use of mind-altering drugs led to many of the musical experiments in psychedelic rock
- Lyrical themes are often surreal, fairy–tale or mystical
- **Concept albums** – songs linked by a storyline or musical theme. Little attempt to produce commercial, radio-friendly, 3-minute pop songs

- The Grateful Dead played their take on country-influenced rock, with long drawn-out instrumental solos, playing festivals and open-air concerts. They remained popular well into the 1990s until the death of singer and guitarist Jerry Garcia
- Frank Zappa and Captain Beefheart were two of the era's most creative and imaginative artists. While some of their music can be described as psychedelic, they also had hard rock, progressive rock and jazz influences. Zappa even released a disco-influenced tune, 'Dancing Fool' (with ironic lyrics) in the 1980s, which had moderate chart success
- The Doors took influences from blues and musical theatre to create their blend of hard rock and psychedelic rock. They were formed in the mid-1960s and wrote many songs that are considered classics, achieving some chart success with 'Light My Fire' (1967). Their sound featured organ and electric piano prominently, and incorporated long, improvised solo sections. Singer Jim Morrison was a controversial character who also wrote poetry, and was often in trouble for swearing at concerts and in confrontations with the police and authorities. He died in 1971, probably of drug misuse.

Progressive rock

INSTRUMENTATION

Drums, bass, guitar, keyboards – synthesisers, electric organ and electric piano, vocals and backing vocals; sometimes strings, horns and world instruments.

PERFORMANCE AND ARRANGEMENT

- Can be musically complex and technically difficult to play. Instrumental virtuosity is important – long, complex instrumental passages
- Melody and harmony is sometimes complicated and unusual – use of **modes** and a classical approach to harmony
- Structures can be complex; long songs with many changes
- Changes in texture and dynamics more common than many other rock styles
- Time signature and tempo changes used; complex time signatures
- Drum parts can be rhythmically complex; use of drum solos.

TECHNOLOGY AND PRODUCTION

- Like the music, the production tried to achieve the highest technical excellence possible – use of **lush reverbs**, delays and expensive-sounding layered recordings
- Guitar sounds covered a large range, from various clean sounds, use of effects like chorus, flanger and phaser to full-on heavy-rock distorted and fuzz sounds
- **Synthesisers** played an important role. Often used for solo work rather than sound effects. Synthesisers like the Moog and ARP were fairly new instruments, but were used extensively alongside other electronic keyboards such as electric organ and electric piano.

MAIN ARTISTS

- Pink Floyd: see below for recordings
- King Crimson: *In the Court of the Crimson King* (1969)
- Yes: *Close to the Edge* (1972)
- Genesis: see the next page for recordings
- Jethro Tull: *Aqualung* (1971)
- Soft Machine: *Volume Two* (1969)
- The Moody Blues: *Days of Future Passed* (1967)
- Emerson, Lake & Palmer: *Tarkus* (1971).

Like psychedelic rock, there were many influences shown and some bands were not exclusively progressive rock.

INFLUENCES

- UK rock of The Beatles, The Who and The Kinks
- Velvet Underground and psychedelic rock
- Jazz
- World music
- Classical.

KEY FACTS AND TERMINOLOGY

- Began in the late 1960s, alongside or as part of the psychedelic rock scene; also known as prog rock
- Continued to be popular and successful throughout the 1970s, though by the end of the 1970s the music was seen as outdated and stale
- Bands were not chart acts releasing singles; they concentrated on albums which were often based on themes or a concept (see psychedelic rock, page 77)
- Many of the bands evolved to have a more commercial sound and some chart success in the 1980s – Pink Floyd, Yes and Genesis included.

PINK FLOYD

Pink Floyd had early success with *The Piper at the Gates of Dawn* (1967) with Syd Barrett as singer. They became a popular band on the festival circuit and the underground alternative scene. Barrett left the band due to mental health problems, and Dave Gilmour took over as singer. In 1973, *Dark Side of the Moon* was released, one of the most widely respected and appreciated albums ever made, and launched the band to international success. Among other themes, it deals with madness and mental health issues suffered by Barrett. Several more successful albums followed in the 1970s, including *The Wall* (in 1979) and the accompanying animated film in 1982.

GENESIS

Genesis also formed in the late 1960s and became popular through the early albums *Trespass, Nursery Cryme* and *Selling England by the Pound*. In 1974 *The Lamb Lies Down on Broadway* was released, a concept album based on a mythical folk tale. It is seen as adventurous and experimental for its musical forms and use of electronics – synthesiser maestro Brian Eno contributed some of the strange noises. Lead singer Peter Gabriel left the band after this, and drummer Phill Collins took over on vocals. The band went on to have more successful releases, including chart hits in the early 1980s, and Phil Collins became a prominent pop artist in his own right in the late 1980s. Gabriel also has a successful career as a producer and performer in world- and electronic-influenced music.

Heavy rock (special focus style 2014)

INSTRUMENTATION

Many bands use two guitarists, drums, bass, vocals (usually male), keyboards.

PERFORMANCE AND ARRANGEMENT

- Vocals are **high-powered**, sometimes very high in register, and almost delivered at screaming levels (e.g. Robert Plant of Led Zeppelin), though can also be rough and lower-pitched
- **Riff**-based guitar patterns; use of **power chords** (root and 5th only)
- **Soloing** that includes fast, technically difficult work
- **Blues-based**, using pentatonic scales and blue notes, or modal scales and chromaticism in the construction of riffs and solos/lead lines
- Driving, insistent rhythms from guitars (**chugging**), drums and bass – sometimes using shuffle rhythms
- Keyboards are fairly common though not often in a very prominent role
- Drum parts feature lots of cymbals and toms and can be very technical.

TECHNOLOGY AND PRODUCTION

- Use of **distortion**, **valve amp** sound, and other effects to create a massive guitar sound central to the whole music
- Use of effects like **fuzz**, **wah-wah** and **phaser**
- Original techniques of performing like **feedback** and **finger tapping**
- Drums and bass are thick and heavy
- Fairly large, obvious reverb is typical.

MAIN ARTISTS

- Jimi Hendrix (see below)
- Led Zeppelin released the albums *Led Zeppelin I, II, III* and *IV* from 1969 to 1971, followed by four more in the 1970s. Well-known songs include 'Whole Lotta Love' (1969), 'Black Dog', 'Rock and Roll', 'Stairway to Heaven' (1971), 'Kashmir' (1975)
- Deep Purple: 'Black Night' (1970), 'Smoke on the Water' (1972), 'Woman from Tokyo' (1973)
- Black Sabbath: 'Paranoid' (1970), *Sabbath Bloody Sabbath* (1973)
- Motörhead: *Motörhead* (1977), *Ace of Spades* (1980)
- Iron Maiden: 'The Trooper' (1983), 'Two Minutes to Midnight' (1984)
- Saxon: 'Motorcycle Man' (1980), *Wheels of Steel* (1980), *Princess of the Night* (1981)
- Def Leppard: 'Bringin' on the Heartbreak' (1981), 'Rock of Ages' (1983)

Bands from the USA included Metallica, Megadeth, Bon Jovi and Van Halen.

INFLUENCES

- Blues
- R&B
- Prog rock
- British blues
- Psychedelic rock.

KEY FACTS AND TERMINOLOGY

- The development of heavy rock owes much to the **blues** and **R&B** of the 1940s–1960s, and is very much about the development of the **electric guitar** as a centrepiece to the music – both as a lead and rhythm instrument
- Guitar-playing bluesmen and rock-and-roll artists like John Lee Hooker, Muddy Waters, B. B. King and Chuck Berry helped make the electric guitar a prominent centrepiece to the sound of popular music
- **Distorted** tone of the guitar characterises heavy rock, and has been influential on all guitarists since it first became used.

JIMI HENDRIX

Jimi Hendrix was one of the most pioneering and influential guitarists in shaping the heavy-rock sound and style. Hendrix started playing R&B in the early-to-mid-1960s in Nashville and New York, having various positions as a session musician (including playing with Little Richard's band). In 1966 he moved to London and formed the Jimi Hendrix Experience, getting rave reviews from fellow musicians and fans for his extravagant gigs, which included playing the guitar behind his head and with his teeth, and on occasion setting light to one of his guitars. His singles 'Hey Joe' and 'Purple Haze' climbed high in the charts, and the album *Are You Experienced* stayed in the charts until the summer of 1969. Tours in the USA and the release of the album *Axis: Bold as Love* followed in 1967.

1968 saw the recording and release of *Electric Ladyland*, with Hendrix now based in the States. It featured longer songs, more of Hendrix's own compositions and guest musicians such as members of Traffic. 'Voodoo Chile' and 'All Along the Watchtower' are two classic songs from the album.

The Jimi Hendrix Experience split in 1969, but Hendrix continued performing with new musicians, calling his band Gypsy Sun and Rainbows by the time they played the legendary Woodstock festival, which included the iconic performance of 'The Star-Spangled Banner'. Tours in Europe and the USA continued, with a confused series of arrangements over band line-ups (now called the Band of Gypsies).

Hendrix died in 1970, just after he had become one of the first artists to open his own studio. Although Hendrix's music was never straight heavy rock, fusing diverse elements of funk, soul, psychedelia and jazz with his heavily blues-fuelled playing, his attitude and style certainly contributed massively to the sound of heavy rock as it developed in the early 1970s.

Other guitarists from the 1960s who took the blues style and made it harder and heavier included Eric Clapton (Cream) and Pete Townshend (The Who), but the next crop of bands to really develop the style included Led Zeppelin and Deep Purple in the early 1970s, and heavy rock started to develop a following and an identity in the UK. Stage acts were extravagant, long and loud. The image was about rebellion, the freedom to be individual and 'live hard, die young'.

Bands such as Kiss, Queen, Thin Lizzy, Alice Cooper and Aerosmith were all successful in the UK and USA in the first half of the 1970s, and adopted the influence of the sound while staying in a slightly more pop-oriented vein. In Canada, Rush's first three albums were very much in the heavy-rock style, and female-led group Heart proved that not all heavy rock was male-oriented. By the mid-1970s, Deep Purple had split up and though Zeppelin's tours were outselling The Rolling Stones, heavy rock was becoming unfashionable.

Newer bands emerging in the late 1970s and early 1980s had less of a blues influence, usually referred to as heavy metal. Examples at this time were Motörhead – a faster, punk-influenced version of heavy rock; and the new wave of British bands that followed at the end of the 1970s, led by Iron Maiden, Saxon and Def Leppard, and Metallica and Megadeth in the USA.

Two major acts emerged at the end of the 1970s – Van Halen in the USA and AC/DC from Australia. Both enjoyed massive worldwide success, with Eddie Van Halen guesting on guitar for Michael Jackson's single 'Thriller', and his own single 'Jump' reaching number one in 1984. AC/DC released the massively successful *Highway to Hell* in 1979 and followed it with *Back in Black* in 1980.

The influence of heavy rock has continued through the decades since the 1980s, though only a few of the original bands still remain active – including Aerosmith, Bon Jovi and Van Halen. Newer styles such as grunge and the many sub-genres of metal are direct descendants of the heavy-rock artists of the 1970s and 1980s.

THE SOUND OF POPULAR MUSIC

Glam rock

INSTRUMENTATION

Vocals (predominantly male) and backing vocals; guitar, bass, drums, keyboards, percussion; sometimes with horns.

PERFORMANCE AND ARRANGEMENT

- **Melodic**, hook-laden catchy songs
- Simple song structures
- **Distorted guitar** playing riffs/chordal patterns based on rock and roll and R&B
- **Driving rock beats**, sometimes using a shuffle rhythm (see blues on page 52)
- **Camp, glitzy** delivery: make-up, sparkly costumes and high-heeled boots; larger-than-life stage personas/alter-egos.

TECHNOLOGY AND PRODUCTION

- Similar to other early 1970s rock productions
- Guitar sounds based on **distortion, fuzz** and powerful amplification
- **Multi-track recording** giving a clear and big sound
- Some use of synthesisers and effects for experimental sounds
- Natural or plate reverbs
- Tape echo.

MAIN ARTISTS

- T. Rex/Marc Bolan: 'Get It On' (1970), 'Jeepster' (1971), 'Metal Guru' (1972)
- Slade: 'Cum on Feel the Noize', 'Mama Weer All Crazee Now' (1972), 'Merry Xmas Everybody' (1973)
- The Sweet: 'Blockbuster' (1973), 'Ballroom Blitz' (1975)
- David Bowie: 'Space Oddity' (1969), 'Starman' (1972), 'Life on Mars?' (1973)
- Bryn Ferry/Roxy Music: 'Virginia Plain' (1972), 'The 'In' Crowd' (1974)
- Roy Wood/Wizzard: 'See My Baby Jive', 'I Wish It Could Be Christmas Everyday' (1973)
- Gary Glitter: 'Rock and Roll (Parts 1 and 2)' (1972), 'I'm the Leader of the Gang (I Am)' (1973)
- Mott the Hoople: 'All the Young Dudes' (1972), 'Roll Away the Stone' (1973)
- Suzi Quatro: 'Can the Can' (1973), 'Devil Gate Drive' (1974).

INFLUENCES

- Rock and roll
- Heavy rock
- Psychedelic rock
- 1960s pop.

KEY FACTS AND TERMINOLOGY

- Popular from 1970 until 1976
- While some glam was intentionally 'disposable', **commercial**, shallow pop music, other artists had a deeper and more **'arty'** approach (Bowie and Bryan Ferry/Roxy Music)
- Glam artists are responsible for two of the most enduring Christmas songs – 'Merry Christmas Everybody' by Slade and 'I Wish It Could Be Christmas Every Day' by Wizzard
- Many glam artists were deliberately androgynous – displaying uncertain sexuality
- Lyrics tended to be light and stayed away from controversial themes, although were often sexually suggestive
- Elton John, Queen and Rod Stewart were other very popular artists who produced music that was influenced by glam, though all were more varied in their style and went on to be successful beyond the glam era.

Slade was one of the most successful bands of the glam scene, and had a sense of humour and lightness about their music. Their sound was closely linked with heavy rock, and they had a big, powerful, guitar-driven sound, yet managed to avoid being too serious and created many commercially successful singles and albums.

DAVID BOWIE

Bowie was an important figure in shaping the glam sound, but his songwriting was often closer to the complex arrangements and structures used by The Beatles and progressive rock bands.

Initially influenced by folk rock and psychedelic rock, Bowie re-invented himself several times throughout a long career at the top of popular music, spanning the 1970s, 1980s and into the 1990s. He adopted different personas – Ziggy Stardust (the 1969 LP *The Rise and Fall of Ziggy Stardust and the Spiders from Mars* is a concept album based on the life of rock star Ziggy), and the Thin White Duke during the 1980s soul- and funk-influenced projects. Later work was more abstract, influenced by **ambient** and **electronic** styles. He worked as a record producer for a number of acts from early in his career, his videos in the 1980s broke new ground and he also acted in several films.

BRYAN FERRY

Roxy Music only made a few albums at the start of the 1970s, and had a strong experimental element through the **synthesiser work** of Brian Eno (who went on to be a big influence in electronic music), and through the use of saxophone, oboe and violin. Bryan Ferry continued as a solo artist and maintained a successful career throughout the 1970s and 1980s, surviving the punk movement and always receiving acknowledgement for originality despite much mainstream chart success.

Disco

INSTRUMENTATION

Vocals (quite often female, but also male), group backing vocals, drums, bass, percussion, guitars, keyboards – particularly electric piano and clavinet, also synthesisers; horn section (using flute, french horn and even tuba in addition to the usual sax, trumpet and trombone); sometimes a string section – generally large ensembles.

PERFORMANCE AND ARRANGEMENT

- **Dance** music with a strict tempo – usually around 120 bpm
- **Four-to-the-floor** (i.e. playing crotchets) **kick drum** gives an insistent relentless beat; hi-hat often plays open **off-beat** quavers; snare (or hand clap) based around beats 2 and 4
- Percussion often busy, using Latin influences; lots of **syncopation**
- Bass lines sometimes melodic and syncopated, sometimes playing root–octave patterns on quavers
- Rhythmic, **choppy** harmony parts from guitars and keyboards
- Horn-section role similar to Motown and soul – instrumental sections, additional harmony and rhythmic stabs
- Vocal melodies based on typical pop song verse–chorus–bridge; emphasis on memorable hooks; exuberant and energetic, sharing many characteristics of soul, such as embellishment of melodies with slides and grace notes
- Chord patterns sometimes very simple, sometimes basing whole sections on a single chord, but often using **extended chords** like 9ths and 7ths.

TECHNOLOGY AND PRODUCTION

- Large-scale **multi-track recording** used for big ensembles; two or more tape machines **sync**ed to give extra tracks
- Big, rich sound – lots of reverb on vocals and horn parts; deep bass; bright with lots of high-frequency content
- Guitar sound clean, bright and thin
- Keyboards – Fender Rhodes and Wurlitzer electric pianos; Hohner clavinet; synthesisers
- Use of **wah wah** and chorus on guitars and also keyboards
- Early use of **sequencers** and **drum machines** – note that at this stage these were **analogue** devices using electrical components, not computer chips
- Popularised the use of electronic **hand claps**
- Kick drum was given deeper sound by **triggering** a low synth note to play in time with it
- Songs released as **12" singles** so mixes would run to 7 or 8 minutes – usually the full song then a remixed instrumental version, but edited together so there was no break in the music. The song could then run for longer in the clubs

- The idea of the **re-mix** was also started here – the extended mix, featuring the instrumental, would include new parts such as percussion and keyboards or solos, or would just re-work the arrangement by removing parts of the mix
- DJs would **beat match** and mix the songs together so there was no break in the beat when starting a new song.

MAIN ARTISTS

- Donna Summer: 'Love to Love you Baby' (1975), 'I Feel Love' (1977)
- Chic: 'Le Freak' (1978), 'Good Times' (1979)
- Earth, Wind & Fire: 'September' (1978), 'Boogie Wonderland' (1979)
- KC and the Sunshine Band: 'Get Down Tonight' (1975), 'That's the Way (I Like It)' (1975), '(Shake, Shake, Shake) Shake Your Booty' (1976)
- Sister Sledge: 'We Are Family' (1979)
- Gloria Gaynor: 'Never Can Say Goodbye' (1974), 'I Will Survive' (1979)
- George McCrae: 'Rock Your Baby' (1974), 'I Get Lifted' (1975)
- The Jackson 5: 'Dancing Machine' (1973)
- Barry White: 'You're the First, the Last, My Everything' (1974)
- Diana Ross: 'Upside Down', 'I'm Coming Out' (1980)
- The Bee Gees: 'Stayin' Alive' (1977), 'Night Fever' (1978)
- Village People: 'Y.M.C.A.' (1978), 'Go West' (1979)
- Boney M: 'Daddy Cool' (1975), 'Ma Baker' (1977), 'Rasputin' (1978).

Many 1970s and 1980s rock and pop acts were influenced by disco, including The Rolling Stones, David Bowie, ABBA and Rod Stewart.

INFLUENCES

- R&B
- Gospel
- Soul (particularly Philadelphia soul)
- Funk
- Latin.

KEY FACTS AND TERMINOLOGY

- Started in gay clubs in New York in the early 1970s, then spread to other American urban centres
- Named after the French name for nightclubs – 'discothèque'
- Lyrics are mainly love songs and party songs
- The complexity of the techniques used in the productions was a sign of producers and engineers becoming more involved in the creative possibilities of technology – it became studio music and pointed the way for other technology-based styles to follow

- Quickly adopted by the pop scene; came to dominate the charts in the mid-to-late 1970s by bands like Boney M, The Bee Gees and Village People
- Disco came to represent everything that was bad about pop music for a lot of rock bands and their fans
- Some of the original American bands such as Chic and Earth, Wind & Fire are highly creditable and have had long and successful careers as writers and producers since the disco era.

By the mid-1970s disco had become the sound of pop music, and its popularity continued until the mid-1980s, though it went into a steady decline from the start of that decade. Donna Summer's 1977 hit 'I Feel Love' – produced by Giorgio Moroder – used a rhythm track completely produced with **drum machines** and **sequenced synthesisers**. This was ground-breaking at the time, though now common practice.

CHIC

As a band they produced several massive hits – including 'Le Freak' and 'Good Times' – and as producers they were behind many disco hits in the late 1970s, going on to produce high profile artists like David Bowie and Madonna.

The bass line/groove from 'Good Times' is possibly one of the most distinctive and well-used in pop music history – sampled on many hip-hop songs and reworked by Queen in their single 'Another One Bites the Dust'.

THE BEE GEES

Three brothers based in the UK who sang close-harmony parts with falsetto lead vocals, a distinctive and unique vocal sound. They were a constant presence in the charts in the 1970s with a string of hits, rivalling sales of some of the biggest selling artists of all time such as Elvis and Michael Jackson. Also provided much of the soundtrack for the film *Saturday Night Fever*, which was based around the disco dancing scene.

Funk

Funk was was the more authentic and underground relative of disco during the 1970s and beyond, with less commercial success but more respect from musicians and discerning fans.

INSTRUMENTATION

Similar to disco; vocals were not always used and tended to be more raucous and R&B-influenced than the smooth sound of disco. Some ensembles were smaller, though horn sections were often used.

PERFORMANCE AND ARRANGEMENT

- Exuberant and energetic – lively, chaotic stage shows
- Drum beats not constrained to the four-to-the-floor of disco; more variation and syncopation, often with intricate, fast hi-hat work and a heavy **backbeat** on beats 2 and 4
- Bass lines syncopated and melodic; development of **slap-bass** technique
- Similar guitar style and keyboard use to disco
- Extended groove-based sections, often with little harmonic variation but plenty of rhythmic interest and punctuation by melodic lines
- Featured improvisation and soloing more than disco
- Rebel, anti-establishment image.

TECHNOLOGY AND PRODUCTION

- Similar to disco, though usually with more focus on the live recording of real musicians and fewer production tricks.

MAIN ARTISTS

- James Brown: 'Get Up (I Feel Like Being A) Sex Machine' (1970), 'Get Up Offa That Thing' (1976)
- Funkadelic: *One Nation Under a Groove* (1978)
- Isaac Hayes: *Shaft* (1971)
- Sly and the Family Stone: 'Everyday People' (1968), 'Family Affair' (1971)
- Stevie Wonder: 'Living For The City' (1973), 'Sir Duke' (1977), 'I Ain't Gonna Stand For It' (1980).

Other funk bands included The Isley Brothers and Kool and the Gang. You will notice that some of the acts are also categorised as soul. Some disco bands such as Chic and Earth, Wind & Fire can also be considered funk bands.

INFLUENCES

- R&B
- Soul
- Jazz (particularly bebop)
- Psychedelic rock
- Latin.

KEY FACTS AND TERMINOLOGY

- Beginning at the end of the 1960s as a development of soul, the main artists listed above were active in the 1970s and early 1980s. The influence of funk continued later into the 1980s through artists like Prince, and influenced many pop acts like Level 42
- In the 1990s, the UK **acid jazz** style borrowed heavily from funk and jazz funk, through artists like Brand New Heavies, Galliano and Jamiroquai.

PARLIAMENT/FUNKADELIC

Singer George Clinton led these bands, who were at the forefront of the funk sound. The two names – often referred to as Parliament/Funkadelic or P-Funk – were in fact the same band, but contractual and legal issues led to to the change in names. They used psychedelic elements mixed with the deep **grooves** of funk, and explored futuristic and sci-fi themes with their lyrics and stage shows.

STEVIE WONDER

As a prolific songwriter and popular artist over several decades, Stevie Wonder embraced the funk style after his success in the 1960s as a soul singer with Motown. His music was varied, and took in pop ballads and more soul-influenced offerings as well as funk groove-based productions. He was one of the major artists of the 1970s and 1980s, doing duets and stage shows with other major artists like Michael Jackson, Paul McCartney and Bob Marley.

JAZZ-FUNK AND FUNK-ROCK

- Developed in the 1970s, using funk grooves with jazz top lines and harmony/chord structures
- Jazz keyboard player Herbie Hancock's *Head Hunters* (1973) was a landmark album
- Jazz trumpeter Miles Davis experimented with this type of fusion
- Weather Report played jazz-funk as well as jazz-rock fusion
- Stanley Clarke was a virtuoso slap-bass player
- Bands such as Jane's Addiction and Red Hot Chilli Peppers used many funk influences in their brand of 1980s and 1990s rock.

Ska, reggae and dub (special focus style 2014)

INSTRUMENTATION

Vocals and often three- or four-part backing vocals; drums, bass, percussion, electric guitar (often more than one), piano, organ, synthesisers, horn section.

PERFORMANCE AND ARRANGEMENT

- Drums emphasise beat 3 – known as the **drop**. The snare – or often sidestick – is played on beat 3 and often has added **syncopated** beats, while the kick varies depending on era and beat. **One drop** has kick mainly on beat 3 (early styles); **steppers** has four-to-the-floor kick drum (used during the mid-1970s); other styles use different kick patterns which often include some syncopation
- Off-beat **chop** on guitar and piano, **staccato** and punchy. Variations include double chop (guitar) and extra on-beat or syncopated chops to emphasise phrases
- Organ **shuffle** or **bubble** – left hand plays off-beat quavers in between the guitar/piano chops. Right hand plays chop on beats 2 and 4 but also snippets of melody, sustained chords and on-beat chops
- Bass usually plays **riff-like** repeated patterns
- Simple, repeated chord patterns, often with few or no changes throughout a song
- Instrumental or harmony parts of horn section or keyboard lines, or sometimes on guitar
- Wide variety of percussion used
- Vocals are often expressive and **soulful**, with improvisation or embellishment of lines, and extensive use of harmony vocals
- Precise and tight rhythmically, but still with a relaxed delivery.

TECHNOLOGY AND PRODUCTION

- **Heavy bass** with plenty of low frequency, heavily **compressed** and prominent in the mix
- Drums recorded with lots of **isolation**, and treated with gates and compression to achieve a separated and punchy sound
- Piano and guitar chops **EQ**ed to sound very thin – pianos often sound unnaturally so. Mixed so they blend together
- Organ shuffle usually mixed fairly quietly; sometimes the left-hand part is barely distinguishable
- The **sparseness** of the playing leaves lots of room for additional guitars and keyboards
- Vocals and horns recorded and mixed with lots of clarity (usually)
- Plenty of reverb used to give a sense of space to dry, close-mic recordings.

DUB MIXING

- **Stripped down** to drums and bass by muting other tracks on the mixing desk
- Snare or sidestick with splashes of large amounts of **reverb** (**spring** or **plate** in 1960s and 1970s)
- Dropping instruments, vocals and horns in and out with **echo** (**tape echo**); often timed delay with high feedback setting
- Large amounts of **reverb** to place instruments far in the distance
- Instruments allowed to 'leak' into the reverb send so there is no dry signal, only effected sound – also happens from leak into drum mics
- **Phasing** or **flanging** applied to sections of the mix or individual instruments
- **EQ sweeps** – manually changing the frequency of a boosted EQ
- **Timed delay** on snare, piano/guitar chops or the hi-hats
- The engineer 'plays' the studio like an improvised performance.

MAIN ARTISTS

- The Skatalites: 'Guns of Navarone' (1962), 'Man in the Street' (1964)
- Alton Ellis: 'Get Ready – Rock Steady', 'Cry Tough' (1966)
- Bob Marley and the Wailers: 'I Shot The Sheriff', 'Get Up, Stand Up' (1973), *Exodus*, 'One Love' (1977)
- Jimmy Cliff: *Wonderful World, Beautiful People* (1969), *The Harder They Come* (1972), 'Many Rivers To Cross' (1972)
- Burning Spear: 'Slavery Days' (1975), 'Black Disciples' (1976)
- Dennis Brown: 'Money In My Pocket' (1977), 'Milk and Honey' (1977)
- Eek-a-Mouse: *Wa-Do-Dem* (1981)
- Gregory Isaacs: *Night Nurse* (1982), 'Rumours' (1988)
- Shabba Ranks: 'Mr Loverman' (1992)
- Damian Marley: 'Welcome to Jamrock' (2005).

UK REVIVAL

- Madness: *One Step Beyond...* (1979), 'Baggy Trousers' (1980)
- The Specials: 'Too Much Too Young' (1980), 'Ghost Town' (1981)
- UB40: 'Food for Thought' (1980), 'Red Red Wine' (1983).

INFLUENCES

- Blues
- R&B
- Gospel
- Soul.

DUB PRODUCERS

- King Tubby: *King Tubby Meets Rockers Uptown* (1976)
- Lee 'Scratch' Perry: *Return of the Super Ape* (1978)
- Scientist: *Scientist Meets the Space Invaders* (1981).

KEY FACTS AND TERMINOLOGY

- From Jamaica, where the music industry started recording local artists in the late 1950s to play on **sound systems** – mobile rigs with huge speaker stacks and powerful amplifiers that play dance music
- **MC**s (Master of Ceremonies) would 'toast' the crowd using a microphone, which evolved into the **toasting** style of lyrical chanting. They were also known as DJs
- Studio owners would have their own sound – based on a pool of musicians, arrangers and songwriters to record and write for many different singers and vocal groups, like the Motown and Stax approach. **Studio One**, run by Coxsone Dodd and **Treasure Isle**, owned by Duke Reid, were the two biggest early studios
- The **ska** style was the first sound to emerge in the late 1950s and early 1960s. It has off-beat chords played by the rhythm section, similar to reggae but at roughly double the tempo. Ska often featured horn sections playing instrumental tunes, like the swing bands from America
- By the late 1960s the beat slowed down and went through the brief **rock steady** period before becoming the **reggae** style
- In the UK the music was enjoyed by the rapidly growing Caribbean community, and had found some favour amongst the white working class by the mid 1960s – particularly with mods and later with the skinheads. Desmond Dekker's 'Israelites' was a UK number one in 1969
- The Roots style – using political, social and Rastafarian themes – came to dominate in the 1970s with artists like Burning Spear, Culture, Israel Vibration, Bunny Wailer and Black Uhuru gaining success in Jamaica and abroad
- At the same time, **dub** mixing came into being. Dub instrumentals, using mainly just drums and bass, were used by sound systems for the DJs to 'toast' on
- In the late 1980s the **dancehall** or **ragga** style emerged – using electronic sounds, and much more aggressive lyrics, concerned with gangsters and crime more than the 'conscious' themes of earlier styles. The style continues to the present day, as well as the roots style which re-emerged during the 1990s

BOB MARLEY AND THE WAILERS

Bob Marley and the Wailers became a worldwide success in the mid-to-late 1970s. After signing to UK label Island, his band released several albums and toured extensively to promote the music. By 1977, when the *Exodus* album was released, they had gained international recognition and were getting regular chart success. Marley became almost a statesman-like figure because of his strong lyrics on themes of oppression, injustice and liberation. He died in 1981.

Other **roots** groups and singers were very popular in the late 1970s and early 1980s, with acts like Prince Far-I, Burning Spear, Black Uhuru and Culture touring extensively.

Lee Perry was an early studio owner who did a lot to develop the career of Bob Marley and the Wailers. He is also one of the foremost dub producers, along with King Tubby and Prince Jammy.

In the UK in the late 1970s, there was a new sound that emerged with bands like the Specials, The Beat and Madness. Playing ska-based tunes, fused with a punk-like energy and approach, the short-lived style nevertheless provided a platform for UK acts like Madness and UB40 to have long careers with much commercial success.

Punk and new wave (special focus style 2012)

PUNK

INSTRUMENTATION

Vocals (mainly male), electric guitar, bass and drums; keyboards used by some bands.

PERFORMANCE AND ARRANGEMENT

- Hard-edged, raw and chaotic – stripped down, small ensembles; basic music with no frills
- Vocals often delivered at shouting level
- Melodies simple, covering only a few pitches or delivered almost as shouted chants
- Backing vocals (when used) are similar; no complex harmonies
- Often based around simple chord structures – three-chord tricks like those used in rock and roll; simple major chords or power chords common
- Fast tempos; drums loud and trashy; lots of cymbals used
- Straightforward rhythms; some simple syncopation
- Songs often short – around 2 minutes long with basic structures; if solos are included they are quick and simple.

TECHNOLOGY AND PRODUCTION

- **DIY** ethic to the production
- Bands used independent small studios and went for a simple, raw **unprocessed** sound. No clever production tricks
- Guitar sounds are often **distorted**, though quite thin and harsh compared to the full tones of heavy-rock distortion and fuzz
- Effects were still used, but producers avoided the polished sound of disco and pop of the era; there was no 'spacey', psychedelic use of effects like delay and flanging, and no lush reverbs.

MAIN ARTISTS

- Sex Pistols: 'Anarchy in the U.K.' (1976), 'God Save the Queen', 'Pretty Vacant' (1977), 'Something Else' (1978)
- The Clash: 'White Riot' (1977), 'Clash City Rockers', 'White Man In Hammersmith Palais', 'Tommy Gun' (1978), 'I Fought the Law', 'London Calling' (1979), 'Bankrobber' (1980), 'Rock The Casbah' (1982)
- The Stranglers: 'Peaches', 'No More Heroes' (1977)
- The Jam: 'The Eton Rifles' (1979), 'Going Underground' (1980)
- The Buzzcocks: 'Ever Fallen in Love (With Someone You Shouldn't've)' (1978)
- Stiff Little Fingers: 'At the Edge' (1979)
- The Undertones: 'Teenage Kicks' (1978), 'Jimmy Jimmy' (1979)
- The Damned: 'Neat Neat Neat' (1977), 'Love Song' (1979)
- The Ruts: 'In a Rut' (1978), 'Babylon's Burning' (1979)
- Siouxsie and the Banshees: 'Hong Kong Garden' (1978), 'Happy House' (1980)

Punk acts from the USA included the Ramones and the Patti Smith Group.

INFLUENCES

- Rock and roll
- Hard rock sound of bands like The Who and Velvet Underground
- Early 1960s pop.

KEY FACTS AND TERMINOLOGY

- Started around 1975 or 1976 in the US and the UK; 1977 was the year punk exploded
- By 1980 most punk bands had split or moved in different directions
- Punk was a reaction against the excesses of technical, highly produced progressive rock; the similarly highly polished disco and 1970s pop; and the 'serious' attitude of heavy rock
- Designed to be **aggressive**, **anti-establishment**, **disposable** music for the people
- Social and political commentary was often the main thrust of the lyrics, often displaying dissatisfaction with the establishment
- Several bands or songs were banned from radio and TV play
- Many bands supported political movements such as The Anti-Nazi League and Rock Against Racism
- Chaotic dancing – **pogo-ing** – and spitting was common amongst fans at gigs
- Equipment and venues often got smashed up at gigs – one of the influences from The Who, as well as drawing on the raw, energetic sound of the 'power pop' songs. Ironically, The Who were dismissed as ageing rockers by punk bands, though The Clash did some gigs with them in the 1980s

- Fashion was important – custom-made clothing covered with zips and safety pins, lots of black, kilts and tartan. Safety pins were also worn as jewellery/piercings
- Hairstyles included the Mohican, often spiked up and dyed bright colours
- The context of **social unrest** in the UK, due to high unemployment and the battle between the unions and government over working conditions and the future of nationalised industries, influenced punk.

SEX PISTOLS

Despite the anarchist image, the Sex Pistols were actually a **manufactured band**, put together by fashion guru Malcolm McClaren. They outraged mainstream society and had wide media coverage – the attitude of punk was summed up by their song 'No Future', portraying bleak prospects for young people in the UK.

The Sex Pistols only lasted for a few years, as did the height of the punk scene, but their effect was dramatic and changed the face of music.

THE CLASH

The Clash produced some of the most respected music of the punk era, and had more **diversity** than most punk bands, writing songs that were heavily influenced by reggae, dub and ska, funk and rap, rockabilly and rock and roll. Their album *London Calling*, which copied the cover design of Elvis Presley's first album, is widely regarded as one of rock's finest. The Clash continued recording into the early 1980s and although the popularity of the band was declining, they continued to make astute political and social commentary central to their music.

THE RAMONES

From New York, the Ramones are often referred to as the first punk band. Similarly to the development in the UK, in the USA there was a reaction against the perceived lack of edge to most pop. The Ramones were an important part of the music scene based at **CBGBs club,** where many other post-punk and new-wave acts developed their sound through live performances.

NEW WAVE

INSTRUMENTATION

Vocals (male and female), backing vocals, guitar, drums, percussion, bass, keyboards.

PERFORMANCE AND ARRANGEMENT

- Adopted much of the punk **DIY** ethic; fairly raw and unpolished
- Wide range of approaches due to varied stylistic influences, from edgy power pop to reggae and disco, so delivery depended on style
- Song writing became more important, with some clever pop songs, but again avoiding the complexity of progressive rock.

TECHNOLOGY AND PRODUCTION

- Similar to punk – the aim was to achieve an energetic and unprocessed sound of real musicians
- The productions were still often a bit more polished than punk
- Use of keyboards and more variety in the arrangements often gave more depth to the sound than was usual for punk.

MAIN ARTISTS

- Elvis Costello and the Attractions: 'Watching the Detectives' (1977), '(I Don't Want To Go To) Chelsea', 'Pump It Up' (1978)
- Ian Dury and the Blockheads: 'Sex and Drugs and Rock and Roll' (1977), 'What a Waste', 'Hit Me with Your Rhythm Stick' (1978)
- XTC: 'Making Plans for Nigel' (1979), 'Senses Working Overtime' (1982)
- Squeeze: 'Cool for Cats', 'Up the Junction' (1979)
- The Police: 'Roxanne' (1978), 'Message in a Bottle' (1979), 'Don't Stand So Close to Me' (1980)
- The Pretenders: 'Stop Your Sobbing', 'Brass in Pocket' (1979)
- Blondie: 'Heart of Glass', 'One Way or Another' (1978), 'Call Me' (1980)
- Talking Heads: 'Psycho Killer' (1979), 'Once in a Lifetime' (1980).

Other new wave acts included The Cars, Devo, The B52s and Graham Parker and the Rumour.

INFLUENCES

- Punk
- Hard rock
- Reggae
- Funk.

KEY FACTS AND TERMINOLOGY

- Started in the late 1970s, gaining popularity as punk's brief explosion came to an end
- Continued into the early 1980s, though many bands and artists went on to have successful careers as pop artists
- Many of the new-wave acts were signed to independent record companies such as Stiff
- The New York club CBGBs was an important venue for new wave, with bands like Blondie, New York Dolls and Talking Heads evolving their sound there through frequent gigs, alongside the punk sounds of the Ramones
- Like punk, new wave had a strong **independence** from the establishment, which included the major record companies as well as the government
- Lyrics dealt with social and political issues – there were a lot of clever lyricists such as Ian Dury and Elvis Costello – as well as more conventional pop themes
- Many of the British new-wave bands did not gain success in the USA, although The Police, The Pretenders and Elvis Costello had moderate chart popularity with a few songs.

Bands like Joy Division, The Cure and Psychedelic Furs emerged towards the end of new wave, and formed a bridge between punk, new wave, the synth pop or new romantic sound and the indie rock sound that emerged during the 1980s.

BLONDIE

Successful in both America and the UK, they used a range of influences from rock and roll, through punk and reggae to disco, fronted by the sweet-yet-edgy vocals of Debbie Harry. In the song 'Heart of Glass', the disco influence includes use of a **drum machine** (plus real drums) and **sequenced** synthesiser.

ELVIS COSTELLO AND THE ATTRACTIONS

Elvis Costello was a singer-songwriter who went on to explore many different styles including country, folk and big-band jazz throughout the 1980s, 1990s and into the new millennium. His early punk-influenced material also took stylistic features of reggae and classic pop.

THE POLICE

One of the most successful of the new-wave bands, The Police used a lot of reggae influences as well as punk and power pop, with inventive guitar work from Andy Summers. Lead vocalist Sting enjoyed solo success as a major artist during the 1980s and 1990s.

IAN DURY AND THE BLOCKHEADS

Again using a wide range of influences including funk, reggae and punk, Ian Dury's witty and smart observational lyrics bear comparison to music-hall singers. The songs often have dramatic stylistic changes and sophisticated arrangements. A victim of polio in childhood, Dury caused outrage with his song 'Spasticus Autisticus', released in 1981 as a statement against the International Year of Disabled People.

TALKING HEADS

Like Blondie, a product of the CBGBs scene in New York, they used heavy funky grooves and electronica influences. A large band, with percussion and several guitars and keyboards. Experimental electronic musicians Brian Eno and Robert Fripp were involved in their early work. Lead singer David Byrne continues to write and perform, often exploring fusions of world music and other styles with funk-driven pop.

Synth pop

INSTRUMENTATION

Drum machines, synthesisers, vocals and backing vocals; guitars and bass sometimes used, especially in later styles.

PERFORMANCE AND ARRANGEMENT

- Often moody and reserved, introspective performances; later sounds were more pop-oriented with up-beat dance rhythms and a happier sound
- Stark, open, **thin-textured** sound in early work; more full and polished in later years
- **Synthesisers** took the role of guitars, bass and other harmony parts from earlier rock styles – use of riffs, melodic hooks, chord patterns
- Use of **synth pads** – sustaining synth chords playing chord patterns or harmony lines
- Drum rhythms often quite **angular**; not always straightforward backbeat

TECHNOLOGY AND PRODUCTION

- The sound of early **drum machines**, and **monophonic** and **polyphonic analogue synthesisers** provided the sonic signature of the music
- **Real-time manipulation** of synthesis settings such as filter cut-off and resonance, LFO (modulation)
- Drum machines had their own built-in **sequencers** for writing the patterns, as did some synthesisers, though they were often played from the keyboard. Stand-alone sequencers also used – the early songs pre-dated **MIDI** so sequencers used an analogue system called **CV gate**
- Return to the use of lush and obvious **reverbs** after the basic production of punk and new wave, including the early digital reverbs
- Use of **delay** and other **effects** – synthesisers did not come with built-in effects like modern keyboards do. Electronic sounds benefit from effects to add depth to the sound.

MAIN ARTISTS

- Ultravox: 'Vienna', 'All Stood Still' (1981), 'Reap the Wild Wind' (1982)
- The Human League: 'Love Action (I Believe in Love)', 'Don't You Want Me' (1981)
- Gary Numan/Tubeway Army: 'Are Friends Electric?', 'Cars' (1979)
- Kraftwerk: 'Autobahn' (1975), 'Trans-Europe Express' (1977)
- Tears For Fears: 'Mad World' (1983), 'Shout', 'Everybody Wants to Rule the World' (1985)
- The Buggles: 'Video Killed the Radio Star' (1979), 'Living in the Plastic Age' (1980)
- Soft Cell/Marc Almond: 'Tainted Love' (1981), 'Torch' (1982)
- Orchestral Manoeuvres in the Dark: 'Enola Gay' (1980), 'Locomotion' (1984)
- A-ha: 'Take on Me' (1984), 'I've Been Losing You' (1986)
- Eurythmics: 'Sweet Dreams (Are Made of This)' (1983), 'Sisters Are Doin' It for Themselves' (1985), 'Thorn in My Side' (1986)
- Duran Duran: 'Girls On Film' (1981), 'Rio' (1982), 'The Reflex' (1984)

INFLUENCES

- Kraut rock
- Disco
- Art rock
- Glam rock
- New wave
- Punk.

Other synth pop bands included: Howard Jones, Heaven 17, Spandau Ballet, Thomas Dolby, Art of Noise, Depeche Mode, New Order, Devo, Yazoo, Frankie Goes To Hollywood, Pet Shop Boys and Erasure.

KEY FACTS AND TERMINOLOGY

- Early pioneers were German band Kraftwerk, who had international hits in the mid-1970s with their songs based entirely on drum machine and synthesiser ensembles. They continued to be an influential band throughout the 1980s
- The first English bands started appearing at the very end of the 1970s and were known as **New Romantics**, offering an alternative to the chaotic sound of punk
- Many of the early bands were short-lived, thrived in an underground alternative scene only, and had limited commercial success – Duran Duran were a notable exception, as were Eurythmics
- Later acts like Pet Shop Boys adopted the electronic sound but made it more pop-friendly, with strong disco influences
- Many synth pop acts were popular in the gay club scene.

KRAFTWERK

This German band started producing music using synthesisers and drum machines in the early 1970s. In 1975, the album *Autobahn* was a success and was followed by *Trans-Europe Express* in 1977. They generated a lot of interest, and were very influential on the development of the synth-pop style and later electronic styles such as **house**. Their producer Conny Plank worked with Ultravox.

GARY NUMAN

As singer, guitarist and keyboard player with Tubeway Army, and later as a solo artist, Numan was influential in his use of guitar effect pedals to alter synthesiser sounds. Tubeway Army's number one hit 'Are Friends Electric?' was one of the earliest successful synth-pop releases. 'Cars' was another number one, from his influential album *The Pleasure Principle*. The recordings were created using the DIY, low-budget independent ethic of punk.

DURAN DURAN

Caused controversy in 1981 with their erotic video for the single 'Girls On Film'. It had to be heavily edited for use on **MTV** and was banned by the BBC. They had a string of hits in the UK and the USA due to MTV exposure, which was becoming an important platform for promoting music. Their music was more pop oriented than many of the early New Romantic bands, and they wrote the theme tune for the James Bond film *A View To A Kill* in 1985.

BUGGLES

A duo of Trevor Horn and Geoff Downes, Buggles had a major hit with 'Video Killed the Radio Star', and not long after the duo joined prog-rock supergroup Yes. Trevor Horn has gone on to become one of the most renowned producers from the UK, working with Frankie Goes to Hollywood, Seal and Robbie Williams amongst others.

EURYTHMICS

The duo of Annie Lennox (vocals) and Dave Stewart (guitar and keyboards) gained worldwide following after their 1983 success with 'Sweet Dreams (Are Made of This)'. They remained popular throughout the 1980s, though by the mid-1980s they were using a full band and had less of an electronic sound, with more soul and rock influences.

PET SHOP BOYS

Coming to prominence later in the 1980s, and having mainstream popularity continuing into the 1990s, Pet Shop Boys were strongly influenced by New York rap, disco and house as well as synth pop. They achieved massive sales for their releases and international recognition. Their work went on to include re-mixes for Madonna. They made use of computer generated imagery in their 1990s videos.

Other pop music in the 1980s

The rapid shifts in style that occurred at the end of the 1970s and start of the 1980s were followed by a decade without many major innovations, though advances in technology – particularly by the end of the decade, the use of **sampling** and new generations of **digital effects** and **digital keyboards**, plus **MIDI** and widespread **sequencer** use – changed the sound of recordings. The influence of synth pop, combined with these rapid advances in technology, led to a lot of electronic sounds, and a general tendency for music to be '**over-produced**' – reliant on impressive sounds, studio effects and tricks rather than focusing on the music.

On the other hand, the decade saw two of the most successful and enduring pop acts to emerge from the USA – Michael Jackson and Madonna.

MICHAEL JACKSON

Already successful during his childhood as part of the Jackson 5 and with solo releases during the 1970s, Michael Jackson's 1979 album *Off The Wall* was a huge landmark. Produced by Quincy Jones, the blend of soul, funk and other influences was supported by excellent songwriting, including contributions from Stevie Wonder and Paul McCartney. 'Don't Stop 'til You Get Enough' and 'Rock With You' were hit singles from this album.

The next album, *Thriller*, released in 1982, is one of pop's all-time classics and remains the best-selling album ever. Building on the relationship with Quincy Jones, there were seven hit singles from the one album, including 'Billie Jean', 'Beat It', and 'Wanna Be Startin' Something'.

Jackson and his management exploited the possibilities of new TV music channel MTV, making slick, artistic videos, and promoted more singles than usual from his albums – four hits from *Off The Wall* and seven from *Thriller*. Previously, bands and record labels usually targeted one or two songs from an album to be used as singles.

He played massive sell-out concerts around the world, with extravagantly choreographed performances, and followed up with the 1987 album *Bad*, also producing seven hit singles.

Jackson was fairly eccentric in his personal life, which he attempted to keep private as much as he could, but he was so famous this often proved difficult to do. He continued making music in the 1990s, though after *Dangerous* (1991) he released less and rarely gave live shows. He died in 2009 as he was preparing for a series of live shows.

MADONNA

Using urban dance and electronic influences, Madonna's first hits were in 1983 with 'Holiday' and 1984 with 'Like A Virgin'. 'Material Girl' and 'Into the Groove' followed in

1985, then 'Papa Don't Preach' (1986), 'Who's That Girl' (1987), 'Like A Prayer' (1989), 'Vogue' (1990) and 'Justify My Love' (1990).

Madonna constantly re-invented and updated her sound and image, choosing the most cutting-edge producers to work with. The tours were always themed stage shows on a spectacular scale. Like Michael Jackson, she exploited the medium of video to sell her music.

Controversy often followed her, particularly due to her use of religious references and imagery. Madonna remained successful through the 1990s, with albums including the William Orbit-produced *Ray of Light* (1998).

Hip hop (special focus style 2013)

INSTRUMENTATION

Vocals (predominantly male) – rapping; drum machine, record decks (turntables), samplers, synthesisers; sometimes with live instruments like guitar, keyboards, drums, percussion, bass, saxophone and other horns.

PERFORMANCE AND ARRANGEMENT

- Based mainly on repeating rhythmic patterns – **loops**
- Melodic elements are usually short motifs
- Use of riffs, often repetitive
- Sometimes no bass line
- Unusual, unique timbres created by **DJs** using **scratch** techniques on **record decks** – this involves manipulating the playback of a record, moving it quickly back and forth, speeding up and slowing down
- Harmonic elements often have little importance; no large-scale chord patterns or complex harmony
- **Rappers** – often several in a group – perform over the **beats** provided by the DJ
- Rap is rarely melodic – emphasis is on intricate rhythmic delivery and phrasing
- Frequent use of **call and response** chants
- Use of **beat boxing** – rappers imitating the sound of drum machines and other instruments vocally
- Songs usually have a verse–chorus type structure, with a chorus based on a refrain with catchy hooks, often delivered by several rappers.

TECHNOLOGY AND PRODUCTION

- Original hip-hop artists used two or more record decks to play instrumental grooves – often drum and bass **breaks** – while mixing in other patterns or short hits from other records

- Later styles also use **samplers** to create loops (e.g. sampled directly from a DJ using decks), DJ **scratching**, and create unique sounds by reversing, pitch-shifting and filtering
- Special effects from synthesisers/non-pitched sound effects
- **Drum machines** used instead of or alongside loops created by DJs
- Music often has a **lo-fi** quality
- Deep bass frequencies – often from kick-drum sounds.

MAIN ARTISTS

- DJ Kool Herc: influential DJ on the early hip-hop scene, but did not release any music that he produced
- Sugarhill Gang: 'Rapper's Delight' (1979)
- Afrika Bambaataa: 'Planet Rock' (1982), 'Renegades of Funk' (1983)
- Grandmaster Flash: 'The Message' (1982)
- Run-D.M.C.: 'It's Like That' (1983), 'Hard Times' (1984), 'Walk This Way' (1986)
- LL Cool J: 'I Can't Live Without My Radio' (1985), 'I Need Love' (1987)
- The Beastie Boys: '(You Gotta) Fight for Your Right (To Party!)', 'No Sleep till Brooklyn' (1987)
- Public Enemy: 'Don't Believe the Hype' (1988), 'Black Steel in the Hour of Chaos' (1989)
- N.W.A.: 'Straight Outta Compton' (1988), 'Express Yourself' (1989), 'Always Into Somethin'' (1991)
- MC Hammer: *Please Hammer, Don't Hurt 'Em,* 'U Can't Touch This' (1990)
- Coolio: 'Gangsta's Paradise' (1995)
- Eminem: 'My Name Is' (1999), 'The Real Slim Shady', 'Stan' (featuring Dido) (2000), 'Just Lose It' (2004)

Other prominent rap artists include: Snoop Dogg, Puff Daddy (P. Diddy), Tupac Shakur, Wu-tang Clan, Jay-Z, Nas, Lil Wayne, The Black Eyed Peas and Kanye West.

INFLUENCES

- Funk
- Disco
- Soul
- R&B
- Reggae – toasters on sound systems, dub
- Scat singing.

KEY FACTS AND TERMINOLOGY

- 'Rap' generally refers to the music, and 'hip hop' to the complete culture surrounding the music
- Started in the mid-to-late 1970s in New York; **block parties** were part of the culture of the young black population in areas like the Bronx, with big speaker

stacks and powerful amps used to play loud dance music. The idea of **DJ**s playing stripped-down instrumental dance records with a **MC** (master of ceremonies) chatting on a microphone is similar to the toasting used by reggae sound systems

- Dancers created a style called **breakdancing** – a combination of gymnastics and dance
- The recording and release of rap songs only started in the late 1970s – until then it was just about the parties
- Rap didn't have much commercial success in the early 1980s, though some songs did become international hits. The sound had an influence on pop music; the way beats were put together, using sampled loops and scratching, was copied by producers. The early sound became known as **old-school** rap
- Run–D.M.C. and The Beastie Boys were some of the first acts to gain consistent chart success in the late 1980s and into the 1990s; their sound used more drum machines and synths than loops taken from records. This era became known as the **golden age** of rap. Many songs had lyrics that dealt with serious issues – the social situation of African Americans, and political issues. Public Enemy was known for this style of hip hop and was successful from the mid-1980s to the early 1990s; their sound was hard, heavy and thick, with edgy rhythms and delivery of raps, to match the gravity of the messages
- This evolved into the much more hard-line stance of **gangsta rap**, which promotes violence against enemies and society in general, and a criminal gang lifestyle. Women are treated as objects to be bought and sold, and pimping is promoted and glorified. Acts like N.W.A. were forerunners of this approach, and made **West Coast hip hop** from Los Angeles a more popular style than the East Coast (New York) dominated previous styles. Dr Dre and Snoop Dogg were also prominent in the West Coast scene. Dr Dre was originally a member of N.W.A., and went on to become one of the foremost producers in hip hop, working with many artists including Eminem
- West Coast hip hop has a smoother, more funk-influenced sound than East Coast hip hop and this helped it achieve more commercial success, which by the early 1990s was becoming widespread and continues currently – rap has been at the forefront of pop-chart success throughout the 2000s.

Indie rock (special focus style 2011)

INSTRUMENTATION

Classic rock band line-up with guitars, drums, bass and sometimes keyboards; vocals and backing vocals.

PERFORMANCE AND ARRANGEMENT

- Guitar as the main harmony instrument
- Guitar sounds commonly associated with indie are often referred to as jangly – a fairly light tone, often using picked, sustained arpeggios with effects
- Vocals are often fairly understated, with a melancholy or introspective feel
- Backing vocals are not usually a big feature, so the music tends to be relatively sparse
- Some songs are long and loosely structured, almost like extended jams around a groove
- Solos do not form a very important part of the music.

TECHNOLOGY AND PRODUCTION

- Guitar amplifiers and effects play a big part in the sound of indie – the light, **sustained tone** and use of **delays** is common in many bands
- **DIY production** ethic; low budget recordings based on simple capture of live performances.

THE SMITHS

In 1983, The Smiths released the singles 'This Charming Man' and 'What Difference Does it Make?', achieving top 30 chart success. Their debut album *The Smiths* reached no. 2 in the UK album charts in 1984. Singles followed in the same year – 'Heaven Knows I'm Miserable Now' and 'William, it was Really Nothing'. There was trouble with the national press as lyrical themes appeared to deal with some taboo subjects.

Their second album, *Meat is Murder*, courted more controversy with its political lyrics, and lead singer Morrisey gave some hard-hitting interviews speaking out against the Thatcher government. In 1986 they got into legal disputes with their label Rough Trade. Personal problems in the band led to more instability. The album *The Queen is Dead* was released, having been delayed by the dispute with Rough Trade. Singles 'Panic' and 'Ask' got more chart success.

Having signed to EMI, The Smiths eventually split up in 1987 with guitarist Johnny Marr leaving, though the album *Strangeways Here we Come* was completed and released.

HAPPY MONDAYS

Their first album, *Squirrel and G-Man Twenty Four Hour Party People Plastic Face Carnt Smile (White Out)*, was released on Factory Records in 1987. *Bummed* was released in the following year as their second album, and the single 'Wrote for Luck' was a hit in the indie chart. In 1990 their most successful album, *Pills 'n' Thrills and Bellyaches*, was released. Mainstream chart success followed for the album and two singles, 'Step on' and 'Kinky Afro'.

STONE ROSES

In 1989 they released their self-titled first album, and the double A-side single 'Fools Gold'/'What the World is Waiting For' had mainstream chart success. The 1992 single 'One Love' charted in the UK top ten, and their second album *Second Coming* was released in 1994. The single 'Love Spreads' reached no. 2 in the UK charts.

SUEDE

Suede started to attract attention in 1992 with two singles, 'The Drowners' and 'Metal Mickey'. In 1993 their first album *Suede* reached no. 1 in the album chart.

BLUR

Their first album *Leisure* was released in 1991, reaching the top 10 in the album charts. Their second album, *Modern Life is Rubbish*, came out in 1993 and marked their change-over from indie band to Britpop.

Other indie bands:

- Pulp: *Different Class* (1995)
- Elastica: *Elastica* (1995)
- The Cure: *Pornography* (1982), *Wish* (1992)
- The Housemartins: 'Happy Hour' , 'Caravan of Love' (1986)
- Joy Division: *Unknown Pleasures* (1979), 'Love will Tear us Apart' (1980)
- New Order: *Power, Corruption & Lies*, 'Blue Monday' (1983)
- The Wedding Present: *Seamonsters* (1991)
- Idlewild: *The Remote Part* (2002).

INFLUENCES

- UK rock of The Beatles, The Who and The Kinks
- Velvet Underground and psychedelic rock
- Punk rock
- Funk
- House.

KEY FACTS AND TERMINOLOGY

- The music often reflected earlier British styles, particularly the edgier guitar-based pop of the 60s and 70s – bands like The Kinks and The Who – though the overall mood was always unique and the darker side of the music prominent
- Independent of the major record companies and having a DIY ethic to the music business, the indie bands built a following on the college and university circuit, and a large number of independent, small to medium-sized venues in towns and cities all over the UK
- Many of the leading acts in the indie scene, such as The Smiths – one of the most influential indie bands – The Stone Roses and The Happy Mondays, came from the Manchester area. The scene that emerged there, particularly associated with the Happy Mondays, The Haçienda nightclub and the Factory Records label, became known as **Madchester**. There was a strong association with the emerging dance and rave scene
- Factory Records was started in the late 1970s by Tony Wilson, and their earlier signings included Joy Division (later to become New Order after the death of singer Ian Curtis), The Stone Roses and Orchestral Manoeuvres in the Dark
- Factory records owner Wilson also ran The Haçienda nightclub and gig venue, where many indie bands played
- Other prominent bands to emerge from the Manchester area included Inspiral Carpets, James and The Charlatans
- The Cure were more of a post-punk band, but adopted the indie approach and had early success that continued throughout the 1980s and into the 1990s. Joy Division and New Order are also significantly different from many indie bands in their sound, using lots of electronic influences, but still share the same independent ethic
- Another significant indie record label was Rough Trade, who were also an independent distributor, handling the nationwide stocking of record shops for many independent labels. They had the punk band Stiff Little Fingers on their label and also signed The Smiths
- During the 1990s the emergence of **Britpop** can be seen as a related though different style. It enjoyed much more success in the mainstream, and tended to be lighter in its themes and more pop-oriented than most indie music. Oasis, later Blur, The Verve and Coldplay were important bands in the Britpop scene
- From America, the **grunge** style of Nirvana and Alice in Chains was becoming influential, and shared the ethos of indie if not the sound
- Many modern rock bands have a strong influence from indie, such as Franz Ferdinand, Arctic Monkeys, Killers and Kaiser Chiefs.

Electronic dance (club dance) (special focus style 2012)

Electronic dance includes many sub-genres such as house, techno, trance, drum 'n' bass, chillout, trip hop and ambient.

INSTRUMENTATION

Drum machine or drum and percussion samples, synthesisers, samplers, turntables, vocals.

PERFORMANCE AND ARRANGEMENT

- **House**, **trance** and **techno** are up-tempo **dance** music, 120 bpm up to around 140 bpm, designed for dancing in clubs and played by **DJs/programmers** rather than musicians
- **Four-to-the-floor** bass drum and hi-hat emphasis on the off-beat quavers (similar to disco)
- Synth stabs or syncopated staccato stabs on piano
- Use of **synth** for **bass lines**, though some tunes have no bass line
- **Synth riffs** and pad chords
- **Samples** taken from a wide range of instrumental music, singing and spoken word/broadcast
- **Anthemic** or epic feel to songs, with rousing melodies over **breakdowns** (with no drums) that build into the re-entry of the drums
- **Rapping** used on some songs; **soul-influenced** vocals common
- Structure built on building up and breaking down textures and rhythmic elements using a range of **loops**, riffs and ostinati
- **Drum 'n' bass** uses frantic, fast, syncopated drum patterns combined with elements of dub reggae and soul, funk and jazz.

TECHNOLOGY AND PRODUCTION

- Use of computer-based **sequencers** to create the music
- Cheap cost of computer-based systems compared to conventional recording technology made music production accessible to many more people than before
- Drum machines or sampled drums – both **loops** and single hits
- **Synthesisers** widely used. Different styles use synthesisers in different ways, or have certain signature sounds or playing techniques associated with the style
- **Sampling** used extensively – sampled vocals common, together with treatments such as stuttering, gapping and pitch-shift
- **Effects** used in a wide variety of ways – delays used for creating new rhythmic elements or adding spatial elements; sounds mangled beyond recognition by extreme processing; long, distant reverbs used.

MAIN ARTISTS

- Early Chicago and Detroit DJs included: Frankie Knuckles, Chip E, Larry Heard and Derrick May.
- MARRS: 'Pump Up the Volume' (1987)
- Coldcut: 'Doctorin' the House' (feat. Yazz and The Plastic Population) (1988), 'Find a Way' (feat. Queen Latifah) (1990)
- Bomb the Bass: 'Beat Dis' (1987), 'Megablast/Don't Make Me Wait' (1988)
- S-Express: '(Theme from S-Express)' (1988)
- Aphex Twin: *Selected Ambient Works 85–92* (1992)
- The Orb: 'Tripping on Sunshine' (1988), 'Blue Room' (1992)
- The KLF: 'Doctorin' the Tardis' (1988)
- Basement Jaxx: 'Red Alert' (1999), 'Where's Your Head At?' (2001)
- Paul Oakenfold: *Bunkka* (2002)
- Fatboy Slim: 'Trippin' on Sunshine' (1994), 'The Rockafeller Skank' (1998), 'Praise You' (1999)
- Moby: *Play* (1999)
- The Prodigy: 'Charly' (1991), 'Out of Space' (1992), 'Voodoo People' (1994), 'Firestarter' (1996), 'Smack My Bitch Up' (1997)
- The Chemical Brothers: 'Setting Sun' (1996), 'It Began in Afrika' (2001), 'Galvanize' (2005).

Other electronic dance artists include. Orbital, Roni Size, Goldie, Groove Armada, Daft Punk, Leftfield, St. Germain, and Trentemøller.

INFLUENCES

- Disco
- Reggae and dub
- Hip hop
- Synth pop
- Soul
- Funk
- Jazz.

KEY FACTS AND TERMINOLOGY

- Beginning during the mid-1980s, the Chicago house party scene used disused **warehouses** for all-night dance events. Other USA urban areas were soon following the trend
- Started gaining popularity in Europe in the late 1980s, with dance parties known as **raves** being held in fields and warehouses; during the 1990s electronic music was very influential in the pop scene, with artists like Kylie, Madonna and Pet Shop Boys drawing on house, techno and trip-hop influences. However, many electronic artists remained outside mainstream chart sales

- Most artists are **club DJs** as well as music producers, and often re-mix other artists' work in their own style
- From the late 1980s, many mainstream pop singles were also released as various dance mixes on 12″ single and CD. Some singles were released on more than four formats to boost sales and therefore success. Some dance mixes bore little relation to the original single
- The house scene in the UK was closely tied to the indie scene – both shared an underground and DIY ethic to music production and sales, and clubs like The Haçienda in Manchester had DJs playing house music and electronic dance styles, as well as many live indie bands. The Ministry of Sound in London established itself as a leading club for the new dance sound
- The clubs on the Mediterranean island of Ibiza were also important venues for playing house, trance and the new styles that emerged, together with venues in France, Italy, Germany and Spain.

FATBOY SLIM

Musician and DJ Norman Cook is a successful producer of electronic dance music, achieving a number of mainstream chart hits. He played bass for The Housemartins during the 1980s, and started DJing and producing electronic music at the end of that decade. He had success with his act Beats International in the early 1990s, but the big hits came in the mid-1990s, by which time he was calling himself Fatboy Slim. He has continued to work as a DJ and also as a producer and re-mixer for many high profile acts such as Blur and The Beastie Boys.

THE CHEMICAL BROTHERS

Also achieving recognition in the mid-1990s, these DJs played alongside many indie and Britpop bands at live shows. Their work includes original songs with and without vocals, film soundtracks, and re-mixes for artists including Fatboy Slim and Kylie.

THE PRODIGY

Named after the Moog Prodigy synthesiser, the heavy, industrial and hard sound of this band has been a constant presence in the UK dance scene since the start of the 1990s. They have enjoyed some mainstream success, but are mostly known for playing clubs and festivals throughout Europe. Very energetic live shows, featuring two vocalists doing a combination of raps and chants.

MOBY

American artist Moby had big worldwide success with the album *Play* released in 1999. He uses a lot of old recordings of blues and gospel music, recorded by Alan Lomax in the early part of the 20th century (see page 52). He has done remix work for David Bowie, Metallica and Britney Spears among others.

Use more down-tempo beats and thinly spaced textures. Production methods are similar to electronic dance.

MASSIVE ATTACK

Pioneered their own unique sound from the start of the 1990s, with sparse, slow grooves and heavy effects use, floaty female vocalists and the soulful voice of reggae veteran Horace Andy. The style is often referred to as trip hop. Massive Attack have had several critically acclaimed albums and some chart success with singles. They continue to produce music and perform sporadically, but from the start they have been inactive for long periods.

The dance music scene is constantly evolving. In the UK several significant new styles have emerged since the 1990s, including trip hop, drum 'n' bass, UK garage and grime.

Timeline of popular styles

1900	1910	1920	1930	1940	1950
New Orleans jazz			Big band/swing		
				Bebop	
					Cool
		Country			
Acoustic blues				Electric blues	
				Rhythm and blues	
					Rock 'n' ro

This table gives an indication of when the main popular styles emerged and gained popularity (dates are approximate).

1960	1970	1980	1990	2000	2010

Free/avant-garde

Fusion

Modern R&B

Heavy rock

Psychadelic rock

Progressive rock

Funk

Glam rock

Punk

Disco

New wave

Synth pop

Hip hop

Indie rock

Electronic dance

Rocksteady

Reggae

Dub

Dancehall/ragga

How to write your answers

 What will I find in the exam?
 What types of questions can I expect?
 How do I actually get the marks?

What you will find in the exam

The examination for *Unit 2: Listening and Analysing* is divided into two sections (Section A and Section B), asking a total of six questions relating to songs on the exam CD.

Section A will contain four questions that can relate to extracts taken from any era or style of popular music from 1910 onwards. The questions will not require depth of knowledge on every pop music style since the early 1900s, but rather a good general knowledge of the important developments in popular music and supporting technology through the 20th century. Section A is worth 40 marks.

Section B will contain two questions relating to the special focus styles for the year of examination. These questions will require more depth of knowledge, including the contribution of the most important artists/bands, any technology strongly associated with the styles and the main musical features (fingerprints) of the styles. It will also contain more extended response questions, giving you the opportunity to show the examiner what you know. Section B is worth 40 marks.

All six questions in the exam will be split into multiple parts testing four main areas:

1. Identifying key musical features
2. Identifying the use of music technology
3. Historical knowledge
4. Practical application of music technology.

IDENTIFYING KEY MUSICAL FEATURES

These questions will test your ability to identify general musical characteristics and devices present in the songs, specifically focussing on the musical elements.

PITCH

Scales; arpeggios; identifying intervals (perfect 5th, minor 3rd and so on); tonality (major, minor, modal, pentatonic); filling in missing notes in printed staff notation.

RHYTHMIC FEATURES

Triplets; swung rhythms; syncopation; specific features of drum patterns; identifying time signatures.

TEXTURE

Particularly with regard to production – how the parts are combined in the song; is the texture dense, sparse, layered?

TIMBRE

Identifying instruments; describing sounds; identifying aspects of attack, decay and tone quality.

TEMPO

Metronome marks (beats per minute); identifying changes of tempo.

DYNAMICS

Identifying general dynamic levels within the song; identifying fades and dynamic shaping within parts and in the overall mix.

STRUCTURE

Recognising the structural elements of the songs (such as intro, verse, chorus, middle 8 and so on); identifying phrase structure.

In addition to the musical elements listed above, you will need to be able to identify specific performance techniques, particularly on electric/acoustic/bass guitar, drum kit and synthesiser/keyboard. Notable developments in performance practice can come up in the exam (such as the development of whammy bar use on the electric guitar, double kick drum techniques, and so on).

IDENTIFYING THE USE OF MUSIC TECHNOLOGY

In this subject it is just as important to be able to spot what technology is being used to produce and manipulate sound as it is to spot the more traditional use of the musical elements. Questions on the use of music technology will require you to identify the following, and to describe their characteristics and impact on the song as a whole:

- Reverb
- Delay/echo
- Modulation effects (chorus, flanger, phaser)

- Dynamic processors (compressor, limiter, gating)
- Pan
- Filtering and EQ
- Sampling and sample manipulation.

HISTORICAL KNOWLEDGE

Most of the historical knowledge required will be tested in Section B, including:

- Performance practice, including specific performing techniques typical of a style
- 'Fingerprints' of a style – specific uses of the musical elements that make the style distinct from others
- Use of technology, especially any effects/techniques particularly associated with a style
- The origin of a style – its roots and influences
- Any styles that have been heavily influenced by the special focus style
- The main artists/bands associated with a style: their contribution to the style; their important albums; how they have influenced other artists/bands; the particular blend of musical elements that makes the artist/band unique or typical of those associated with the style.

A full list of the artists/bands to be studied for the special focus styles is published on the Edexcel website (www.edexcel.com) at the start of the academic year. This should appear in the section GCE from 2008 > Music Technology > Teacher Support Materials.

Remember that artists generally dislike being put into a box and neatly labelled as being in one style or another, so it is likely that only part of their discography will sit comfortably within the special focus style. These are the albums that should be studied in more depth.

Section A will require enough knowledge of the development of music technology alongside the history of popular music so as to be able to make educated guesses at the decade of recording of any given piece of music, even if it is unfamiliar.

PRACTICAL APPLICATION OF MUSIC TECHNOLOGY

This is the body of knowledge that you have accumulated while completing your practical work. You will have learned various microphone techniques, recording skills, sequencing techniques etc. while you have been working at the music technology portfolio, so all you have to do is apply what you have learned to the scenario presented in the exam paper.

> To recap your knowledge of different microphone types and techniques, see pages 43–51 of the *AS/A2 Music Technology Study Guide* (Rhinegold, 2009).

Typical questions could include:

- "How would you mic up a _____ ?" This type of question may include a scenario such as a live or studio recording.
- "What sequencing techniques might be used to replicate this playing technique?"
- "Describe two features of the recording that could be improved and suggest ways in which you might use processors and effects to do so."
- "How might you thicken the vocal sound in the chorus?"

The types of questions you can expect

The exam style will remain the same from year to year, including a mix of different question types. Each type requires a specific approach in order to increase your chances of gaining maximum marks.

MULTIPLE CHOICE

There will always be a correct answer and (probably) an obvious incorrect answer. If you are unsure of the correct response, eliminate the options one by one in a logical fashion. If you spot an overall pattern in multiple choice responses (e.g. A A B B C C D D), this is completely by chance – Edexcel never arrange the answers like this deliberately. The options are always listed in alphabetical, numerical or some other obvious order.

Put a cross in one box only – never give multiple responses or you will get zero marks. If you make a mistake filling in your answer, make it really clear what the your response is supposed to be.

SINGLE-WORD RESPONSES (AND FILL-IN-THE-BLANKS QUESTIONS)

The examiner is not trying to trick you – if the answer seems obvious, then it probably is!

Do not try to justify a one-word response or explain your answer. Make a considered response to the question, using appropriate musical or technical vocabulary when appropriate and then move on to the next question.

SHORT RESPONSE

These may appear as questions with one or two lines in which to present your answer. The amount of lines given is an indication of how full your response should be. Make a careful note of how many marks are awarded for the question – this will let you know how many points you need to make (this may also be indicated in the question, probably in bold type). **Do not waffle** – keep everything factual and to the point. If there are any words in bold type in the question then you **must** refer to them in your response or it is unlikely that you will score any marks.

EXTENDED RESPONSE

Almost all extended response questions are in Section B, so they are mostly testing your knowledge of the special focus styles. Keep your responses to the point. Unless it is clearly stated otherwise, bullet points are perfectly acceptable and examiners will always prefer them to waffling, padded prose.

TABLE COMPLETION

These are the same as short response or single-word questions, but presented to make it slightly easier to see exactly what the examiners are looking for. Ensure that your responses are in the correct columns. Tables are often given with an example row shaded at the top of the table. Try and use the same sort of language in your responses, with the same amount of depth and technical vocabulary.

STAFF NOTATION/COMPLETE THE MELODY

Melody completion will be presented as staff notation with several notes missing. You are required to fill in the missing pitches. It is the notehead that the examiner is concentrating on – the rhythm is unimportant unless stated otherwise in the question. As such, it is important that the notehead is clearly on the line or in the space you are aiming for – if it is not clear where the notehead should be then you will receive no credit.

Complete this question in pencil initially so that you can make any corrections without making too much mess, then fill in your final response in pen. If you do make a mistake that cannot be corrected clearly, write in the pitch names underneath the stave to make clear what you meant.

COMPLETE THE RHYTHM

Rhythmic dictation will normally be presented as a single percussion line on which you need to write the correct note durations. In this case the pitch is unimportant, so keep all the noteheads on the line. Sometimes rhythms are presented as multiple choice questions, in which case you treat them in the same way as any other multiple choice question.

If the rhythm question involves an element of pitch (e.g. a bongo part), then clearly notate which is the higher note and which is the lower note.

Notation questions will not carry too many marks, so if there is a 'complete the melody' question, any rhythmic questions are likely to be presented in a simpler fashion and vice versa.

ANNOTATE THE DIAGRAM

Panning questions are often set with answers in the form of a diagram. In these questions, you must place the instruments in the boxes appropriate to their position in the stereo field.

Other questions may be presented in the form of a diagram or a track list. For example, there might be a fake sequencer arrange window in which you annotate various aspects of the instrumentation, timing, use of controllers/pitch bend and so on.

How to gain marks in extended response questions

Most of the extended response questions will be found in Section B of the exam, where you will be tested on your knowledge of the special focus styles.

SPECIAL FOCUS STYLES

Year of exam	Special focus style 1	Special focus style 2
2009	Rock and roll	Rap and hip hop
2010	Reggae	Heavy rock
2011	Soul	Indie rock
2012	Punk and new wave	Club dance
2013	Rock and roll	Rap and hip hop
2014	Reggae	Heavy rock

Each special focus question (questions 5 and 6) will be split up into several parts. Some of these will be a mixture of shorter response questions including multiple choice, table completion etc., but there will always be at least one extended response question as well. You will be asked about the historical background/influences, the important artists in the style or some aspect of how music technology is used in the style. You may also be asked more general listening questions about the specific track on the exam CD.

The following are examples of the type of extended response questions you might be asked.

EXAMPLE 1

Referring to specific tracks to illustrate your response, describe how **one** *of the following artists contributed to rock and roll music. (4)*

Chuck Berry   **Eddie Cochran**   **Jerry Lee Lewis**

To answer this question you **must** explain how your chosen artist has contributed to rock and roll music – why he was an iconic figure in this style.

Think about:

   What made him stand out from the crowd?

- Why did he have the label 'rock and roll' attached to him?
- What sort of playing/singing techniques did he develop that were unique, particularly creative, new or specific to the style?
- Did he introduce any new technology to the style?
- Did this artist have some clever marketing techniques?
- Did he reach a new audience?
- Did he take a previously existing style and change it in any way to create the new style? If so, how?
- Are there any specific historical comments you can remember about this artist that are relevant to the question (for example, "he was credited with recording the first rock 'n' roll record")?
- How else did this artist contribute to the style?

It is important to refer to songs by your chosen artist to give examples of what you are trying to say. Simply talking about the artist's background and personality is not going to attract any marks. The examiners will have a mark scheme consisting of lots of statements about the artists arranged as a list of bullet points. Your task is to try and get four of the bullet points on the mark scheme into your answer, getting four ticks and thus four marks. Examiners do not like waffle or padding. Get straight down to tackling the meat of the question without any preamble or introductions.

EXAMPLE 2

It would be very unusual for hip hop and rap music to have complex structures and textures that change frequently. How has Snoop Dogg created structural and textural contrast in this track? **(4)**

This is a very different type of question and highlights several important things you must focus on:

- The question says *"in this track"*, so focus **only** on the recording on the exam CD.
- It is **not** asking anything about Snoop Dogg's background or context – the question is asking about how some musical elements have been used in this particular track.
- The question starts with a scene-setting sentence. This gets you into the right frame of mind to tackle the question itself. In this case it is saying that there probably isn't a great deal of dramatic contrast in this track, so it is setting you up to look for more subtle changes.

This question shows that it is not enough just to learn lots of facts about the special focus styles and the major artists – it is equally important to listen to the music and be able to describe it under the headings of the different musical elements.

Questions could be asked on:

- Harmony/tonality
- Rhythmic features including drum programming (if appropriate)

- Tempo and groove
- Texture
- Timbre – the instruments used, describing the 'sounds' of the style
- Performance techniques
- Structure
- Use of technology.

Again, the examiner will have a list of things to look out for, so it is your task to try and find four of the bullet points on the mark scheme. The mark scheme will contain the most obvious points, so do not feel that the examiner is trying to trap you. If in doubt, start with the things you are most sure of and add the things you are less sure of at the end. It is good practice to make five points for a four-mark question just in case one of them doesn't quite hit the spot.

EXAMPLE 3

Describe **five** elements of reggae music that you can hear in this track. You should refer to the **rhythm, harmony, performance** and/or **production** in your answer. (5)

As with the previous question, this one is asking about the track on the exam CD. Do not discuss reggae in general – focus only on what you can hear in this track.

Here is an example of a possible student response:

The bass guitar has a heavily syncopated rhythm every 2 bars. The drumbeat is simple, using just a bass drum, hi-hat and tom. Notes in the bass line are accented on the 2nd and 4th beats of each bar. The lyrics refer to political issues/beliefs/feelings of the artist.

This response is only worth 1 mark (for 'the drumbeat is simple'). The student just misses the mark on several points because the answer is unclear. For example, what does the first sentence really mean? It could mean that it is a syncopated two-bar riff, but where? The bass-guitar riff changes and one of them isn't really syncopated at all. The student doesn't actually say that the riff repeats every two bars, which is a shame, because if he had done he would have gained another mark for saying 'repeat/repetitive'. The sentence about the accents on the second and fourth beats of the bar sounds correct since this is reggae, but it refers to the bass part which just isn't true of this track. Mention of lyrics in a question of this type rarely gains credit unless the lyrics directly answer the question or the lyrics are referred to in the question itself, which in this question just isn't the case.

A better response would be:

Off-beat chop on guitar
Prominent bass and kick drum on 2nd and 4th beat
Jamaican accent singing
Slow tempo – approx 75bpm
Happy, laid back performance

This response gets 5 marks, even though it is much shorter! It avoids waffle and just lists the important points.

The marks were awarded for: off beat (1), chop (1), prominent bass (1), kick drum on second and fourth beat (1) and laid back sound/slow tempo (1). Note how this student was specific as to how things were used – he specified a tempo in bpm and mentioned what could be heard (i.e. the kick drum) on beats two and four.

Neither response referred to the harmony or production, but the second one still managed to gain full marks. This would not always be the case however, so it is good practice to try and refer to **all** the 'suggestions' in the question just in case the mark scheme says that you can only get a maximum of 2 marks for any one element (such as performance).

EXAMPLE 4

Referring to important artists and styles, discuss how reggae has developed from the 1960s to the present day. **(5)**

In this question it is important to note that you have to refer to an **artist** and a **style**. To ignore this would limit you to a maximum of 3 marks for not actually answering the question. In the previous question it said "you **should**" – so if you didn't refer to all four areas, it is possible that you could still gain full marks (as our second student did), but in this question the language is more direct and commanding – it just states what you must do ("Referring to important artists and styles").

Reggae was made 'most' famous by the artist Bob Marley who sang Baby No Cry. His style was a typical reggae sampled drum beat, either one-drop, steppers or rockers and he used a lot of multitracking, reverb, compression, harmonised vocals and panning.

This response gains 2 marks: Bob Marley (1) and one-drop (1). It is a typical example of a student who continues answering the previous question; this student is still talking about performance techniques, rhythms and production elements rather than the development of reggae. In a sense, he flukes the two marks just by mentioning Bob Marley and one drop, but he hasn't understood what the question is really asking for.

Reggae music was created mainly from styles such as ska and rocksteady. Jamaican record producers such as Coxsone Dodd also owned their own sound systems and encouraged local musicians to record tracks for them. Bands such as the Skatalites and the Wailers were famous for their energetic ska beats. Rocksteady artists such as the Gaylads helped to fuse the two sounds together to create reggae. Artists such as Bob Marley and Jimmy Cliff pioneered this style, helping it gain popularity overseas, so that bands like Madness and UB40 could enhance the genre, up until the present day.

For this question, there is a maximum of one mark for a style and one mark for an artist, so the rest of the marks are allocated to points about how reggae developed. This student has listed several artists and styles, but did so in a way that shows how reggae developed, clearly grasping the crux of the question. For this kind of question it is often better to write in sentences because it helps to organise the flow of thought, but it would still be possible to gain full marks with well-organised bullet points.

This response gained the full 5 marks: listing the styles (1), listing the artists (1), sound systems (1), created mainly from styles such as ska and rocksteady (1), helping it gain popularity overseas so that bands such as Madness and UB40… (1).

Although the response gained full marks, it would have been better had the student not assumed the basics – they mentioned Jamaican record producers, but didn't actually mention that reggae comes from Jamaica. Also, it would have been better had they organised their response a little better instead of going off at a tangent in the middle.

EXAMPLE 5

*Choose **two** artists from the list below and describe their contribution to heavy rock.* **(6)**

Jimi Hendrix   **Van Halen**   **Heart**

This is a similar question to the first one we asked, but is now split into two sections (worth 3 marks each). The rules for tackling this question are the same as before, except that the question no longer asks for specific track references.

Jimi Hendrix

He made very complex guitar solos to fit on the pentatonic scale this made him very good at playing with bands and he would produce very good solos. He would also move around the stage so that he was front of stage. This brought guitar players to the front of stage.

Van Halen

Their guitarist made very complex guitar rhythms. They were also famous for their onstage antics during their live performances. In their performances they used very loud amps. They were one of the first bands so they set the way for others to follow. As they were founded in 1976. Their drum rhythms were also fast and complex.

As you can probably tell, this response is not very strong – it gained one mark for the references to guitar technique and complex solos in the Hendrix paragraph, and even this mark could be argued to be too vague to be creditworthy. The Van Halen paragraph contains no creditworthy points and includes some inaccurate and over-generalised information. If you are going to make a statement about rhythms (or any musical element), you need to be specific about it – for example, 'the rhythms are highly syncopated', or 'the rhythms include lots of fast semiquaver passages alternating with swung quavers'.

Jimi Hendrix

Jimi Hendrix was an American guitarist who pioneered different ways of playing the guitar and performing to a crowd. He played with his teeth also with the guitar behind his back. He also created different effects which can enhance the sound of the music. He is said to be the greatest guitarist of all time and is said to be the inspiration to many of the guitarists today.

Heart

Their use of heavily distorted guitar with a 'chugging' rhythm influenced many heavy metal to do the same. Alongside this, their use of more complex drumming and aggressive raw vocal were particularly influential.

This response gained 3 marks for the first paragraph: played with his teeth (1), use of effects (1), inspiration to many of the guitarists today (1)

… and 0 marks for the second.

Heart was probably the hardest choice from the three options, highlighting the importance of making the right choice if an option is presented to you. Before you answer this question, ask yourself how many really influential, important or unique things can you think of that each act brought to the musical table.

For Heart, a better answer (scoring the full 3 marks) would be:

The band was fronted by a female singer and female guitarist, which was unusual, certainly in the 70s, helping to pave the way for future female-fronted rock bands. Also, they combined folk elements into their brand of heavy rock (they were influenced by Led Zeppelin themselves), especially with their earlier albums and, later on in their career, combined elements of pop into their heavy rock anthems.

Before you start to write your answer for extended response questions…

1. Take a minute to read and re-read the question, noting down what it is really asking you to do.
2. Don't just write anything you can think of – focus on what you are being asked to write about.
3. If you are presented with a choice of artists to answer a question on, take a little time to think through the possible answers you might have for **each** option (even if you think there is an immediately obvious choice), and choose the one you think has more going for it.
4. Plan what you are going to say and think how you can best order your points.
5. Even if something seems obvious, say it anyway if it is accurate and relevant.

Top 10 tips for success in your exam

Revision

1: CREATE A TIMELINE

Collect together your information on the development of different styles and technologies.

- Put together in one place, in short bullet points, the important developments in each decade – just the main points
- Put the decades up on your wall in chronological order.

2: SPECIAL FOCUS STYLES

Make a short list of the style 'fingerprints' for each of the special focus styles.

List the ten most important features for each of the recommended artists/bands including:

- One or two important albums
- One or two important tracks
- How they contributed to the style (three or four points)
- Who influenced them (one or two artists/bands)
- Who they influenced (one or two artists/bands).

3: PERFORMANCE AND RECORDING TECHNIQUES

List some of the performance techniques for some common instruments (e.g. electric guitar, drum kit).

Write a short paragraph (about four lines) on how you would mic up each of the following (including mic choice, positioning and distance):

- A grand piano
- An upright piano
- An acoustic guitar
- An electric guitar
- A bass guitar
- A drum kit
- A large ensemble (e.g. orchestra/choir)
- A small ensemble (e.g. a string quartet)
- Individual orchestral instruments
- Individual percussion instruments (e.g. djembe).

4: GLOSSARY OF TERMS

Copy the words from the glossary onto a spreadsheet, leaving enough space for definitions.

- Print out a copy of your 'undefined glossary' and see how many definitions you can remember without looking up any resources
- Mark your work and find out what you couldn't remember
- Repeat the process, starting with the terms you forgot or got wrong the first time round.

5: LISTENING LOG

Set yourself the task of listening critically to several recordings each week.

- Focus on one area every time you listen e.g. use of reverb, performance techniques or structure
- Write your answers in a book dedicated to this task
- Use appropriate vocabulary in your log.

6: LEARN YOUR MUSICAL VOCABULARY

When you are describing the music in your listening log, did you have the vocabulary to describe what you wanted to say? If not, look up the words and write them in the back of your book with definitions.

7: NOTATION

- Practise identifying melodic intervals
- Practise writing out some simple rhythms you hear in songs that you know – do this from memory
- Practise the 'fill in the missing pitches' questions
- Try to identify scales, modes and arpeggios in the music you listen to
- Practise identifying the tempo (in beats per minute) for songs that you hear.

Exam technique

8: BE FAMILIAR WITH THE LAYOUT OF THE PAPER

Do some practice papers – get your hands on any past papers you can, so that you can see how they look. This way, you won't be taken by surprise.

9: IT'S ALL ABOUT TIMING

- Assign a set amount of time for each section (approximately 50 minutes for Section A and 50 minutes for Section B)
- Assign a set amount of time for each question (approximately 12 minutes for each of the Section A questions and 25 minutes for each of the Section B questions)
- Do not spend too long on one question. If it's a struggle, move on and come back to it later, if you have time.

10: DON'T PANIC!

- Keep a clear head at all times
- Get a good night's sleep the night before your exam and eat properly on the morning of your exam
- Drink plenty of water, but not so much that you need to take too many breaks during the exam!
- If you struggle with one question, it's not the end of the world – don't let it put you off the next one
- You know a lot of stuff! Just show the examiner what you know
- Don't leave any blanks – if you aren't sure, take an educated guess.

Test yourself

Answer the following questions to check how much of this revision guide you have absorbed.

PART 1: MICROPHONES AND MIC TECHNIQUES

1. List three advantages and three disadvantages to using a dynamic microphone.

Advantages	Disadvantages

(6)

2. Describe how you would capture the sound of a grand piano in a studio setting. You should refer to mic choice, placement and direction in your answer along with any other aspects you consider to be important.

....

....

....

....

....

(4)

3. Make **three** points describing some of the difficulties involved in recording a live band and how you would overcome them.

Difficulties	Solutions

(6)

PART 2: EFFECTS AND PROCESSORS

4. List **four** different types of reverb.

i. ....

ii. ....

iii. ....

iv. ....

(4)

5. Name **three** of the main parameters available on a compressor.

i. ....

ii. ....

iii. ....

(3)

6. List **three** ways you could brighten up a dull vocal.

i. ....

ii. ....

iii. ....

(3)

7. Describe how you could re-master a 1930s recording using modern mastering tools.

....

....

....

....

....

(4)

PART 3: SPECIAL FOCUS STYLES

8. Outline the development of club dance music from the 1980s to the present day.

....

....

....

....

....

....

....

....

....

....

....

....

(6)

9. Choose **two** artists from the three given below and describe their contribution to soul. You should refer to at least one album/track by each artist.

Aretha Franklin   *Otis Redding*   *Stevie Wonder*

....

....

....

....

....

....

....

....

(4 for each artist)

10. Describe **five** of the 'fingerprints' of punk music. You should refer to rhythm, performance techniques, harmony and production in your answer.

....

....

....

....

....

....

....

....

....

....

....

(5)

There will also be a number of listening questions in your exam (see the chapter on 'How to write your answers'), referring specifically to the recordings on the exam CD. If you have learned the information in this guide, it will be much easier to spot the instruments, performance techniques, style 'fingerprints' and the use of effects and processors that would commonly be expected in each style.

This guide is not aimed at asking the typical listening questions, but Rhinegold Education also publishes a set of listening tests so you can become familiar with the style of questions common in the exam. These are available in the *Edexcel AS/A2 Music Technology Listening Tests, 2nd edition* book and accompanying CD. You will be asked questions which require you to spot some of the instruments and effects listed in the chapter 'The sound of music technology', so take your time to familiarise yourself with the given examples.

Other than the direct listening questions, you can expect questions like those given in this chapter that require knowledge of popular music since 1910, particularly the special focus styles for the year of your exam. Questions 8–10 on pages 130–131 are typical of the longer response questions you might see in questions 5 and 6 of the exam. Instead of just answering the questions given above, ask yourself the same three questions of each of the special focus styles you have to study. Replace the three artists with three other, randomly chosen artists or bands from the list published by Edexcel.

Similarly, it is likely that there will be a question on mic technique, so ensure you have prepared answers for the more common instruments that are recorded in a band context (such as electric guitars, drums and so on) as well as a few orchestral and acoustic instruments.

Glossary

ADT Automatic **double-tracking**. A tape delay is used to simulate **double-tracking** using only one recording.

Aliasing A usually unwanted artefact that occurs when the sampling rate (in an analogue-to-digital conversion) has been set too low. The term is also often used to describe any electronic introduction of artefacts to a sound.

Analogue Continually changing voltage or current that represents a sound – the representation of the sound is analogous to the original sound wave.

Anechoic chamber A room, insulated from any external vibrations or noise, that is designed to stop reflections of sound, thus preventing any reverberation.

Arpeggiated A chord whose notes are played in succession is arpeggiated. On many synths/keyboards an arpeggiator can be set to sound notes that are held down simultaneously in a particular order or pattern.

Artificial harmonics A playing technique on guitar and other string instruments. Fretting a note with the fretting hand while simultaneously touching a node point to create a harmonic and plucking the string with the plucking hand.

Attack 1) The initial portion of a sound – the time taken for a sound to reach its maximum amplitude.

2) The time taken for a processor to act after the signal has passed a set **threshold**.

Balance The volume of instruments or parts relative to each other.

Beat-matching A DJ performance technique: changing the tempo of the next song to match that of the currently playing song by means of changing the pitch or time-stretching.

Bit depth The number of bits available to describe a number. The more bits, the more resolution will be available. For example, four bits will allow 16 different values while 16 bits will allow 65,536 different values. In audio, a lower bit depth increases hiss and produces grainy audio because the steps between one value and another become audible.

Bottleneck A slide used in guitar playing.

Centre frequency The frequency at which a band-pass or notch filter will have the maximum effect.

Clipping Exceeding the maximum volume specification of a given device. Digital clipping produces a particularly unpleasant sound, but clipping in an analogue device is sometimes acceptable or even desirable.

Cut-off frequency The nominal value at which a filter has an audible effect on the frequency range of a sound. Normally applied to low-pass filters, in which case the cut-off frequency describes the highest audible frequency.

CV/gate Control voltage/gate: used in analogue systems as a means of controlling external devices from a sequencer. The control voltage usually controls the pitch and the gate (sometimes called the trigger) controls the note on/off.

DAW Digital audio workstation (e.g. Logic or Cubase).

Delay An effect in which the original signal is repeated one or more times. There is normally a progressive decrease in the volume and sometimes the high-frequency content with each repeat.

Digital effects Effects units that process the audio digitally. Units often have the ability to apply more than one type of effect at the same time (multi-effects units).

Double-tracking Recording (overdubbing) a nearly identical version of an existing track to be played back at the same time as the original so as to create a thicker sound.

Drawbars Controls used to mix the waveform ratios in a tonewheel organ such as the Hammond B-3.

Echo chamber A large, enclosed space with hard surfaces used to create echoes and reverberation.

Echoplex A tape delay effect.

EQ Equalisation.

Fairlight CMI An early digital sampling synthesiser.

Feedback When the sound produced from a loudspeaker is picked up by a microphone or pickup, amplified further and passed out of the loudspeaker again, forming a loop. It will be heard as an audible frequency.

Frequency modulation Where the frequency of a carrier signal is varied in accordance with a modulating signal. In audio, the carrier and the modulating signal are both in the audible frequency range, creating a complex waveform.

FX Short for 'effects'. Processes applied to a signal to alter its sound quality in some way, or the devices used to do so.

Gain The stage of a pre-amplifier that boosts the level of a signal at the beginning of the signal path. A term commonly applied to any volume boost in the signal path.

General MIDI (GM) An agreed standard to ensure compatibility between **MIDI** equipment manufacturers. The term is now often used just to refer to the agreed list of 128 voices in the GM soundset or to the agreed standard for a set of drum/percussion sounds contained within MIDI compatible sound sources.

Gigasampler A software sampler.

Glitching Glitching occurs when audible, unwanted artefacts are introduced to a signal.

Harmoniser An 'intelligent' pitch-shifter; it follows the pitch of the input audio and adds another pitch, taken from a pre-selected key/scale. Harmonisers will usually be able to add several different notes from the chosen key/scale. Vocalists will often use these devices when performing live to create the illusion of several singers.

Legato Italian for 'smoothly': performing a melodic line without a noticeable break between notes.

Leslie speaker A rotating speaker within an enclosure. Most often used in conjunction with the Hammond organ, which creates a phaser-like effect by means of the Doppler effect.

LFO Low-frequency oscillator: normally applied to a signal to modulate it in some way.

Lo-fi Low-fidelity sound: a recording that is deliberately noisy and lacking full frequency range.

Loop A repeated passage. Often used to refer to samples that are imported into a sequence and repeated.

Mellotron An early, tape-based, sampling keyboard instrument.

MIDI Musical Instrument Digital Interface: An 8-bit computer language developed to allow electronic musical instruments to communicate with each other and the hardware necessary to facilitate this communication.

Modular synth A synthesiser (usually analogue) made up of separate sections (such as oscillators, filters and envelope generators) that are linked together by signal cables.

Mono Monophonic sound: a signal carried on one channel (in stereo systems the same signal would be heard on each channel).

Monophonic 1) A word used to describe a musical texture in which there is only one part.

2) A synthesiser capable of playing only one note at a time is called a monophonic synthesiser.

Musique concrète Music created by capturing, manipulating and combining naturally occurring and artificial sounds on tape.

Normalising The process of boosting an audio signal so that the loudest peak registers as 0dB.

Output gain Signal boost after processing.

Overdub The process of adding additional tracks to previously recorded material.

Palm-muting A guitar playing technique: the notes are muted by placing the heel of the hand lightly against both the strings and the bridge.

Pan The placement of sound in the stereo field.

Plug-in A computer program written to produce or manipulate audio within an existing audio sequencing package.

Polyphonic 1) A word used to describe a musical texture in which two or more musical strands are heard simultaneously.

2) A synthesiser capable of playing more than one note at a time is called a polyphonic synthesiser.

Portamento A gliding effect between changing notes (rather than an abrupt change from one pitch to the next).

Q The range of frequencies affected by a filter – a measure of the resonance of a filter.

Ratio A parameter on compressors used to set how much a signal is reduced by after it passes the **threshold** level.

Regeneration A parameter on flangers used to set the amount of the affected signal sent back into the input.

Release 1) The final portion of a sound – the time taken for a sound to decay after the note has been released.

2) The time taken for a processor to stop acting after the signal has passed a set **threshold**.

Resonance In filters, this is often interchangeable with 'Q', referring to the bandwidth of frequencies allowed to pass or the level of amplification of the cut-off frequency. In acoustics, it refers to the point at which the sound intensifies as it reaches the same frequency as the natural vibration frequency of the air in a space.

Rhythmicon The first example of an electronic drum machine.

Rumble filter A high-pass filter set to eliminate unwanted low frequencies such as footsteps and traffic noise without unduly affecting the wanted portion of the sound.

Sample A short, pre-recorded sound used in the context of a piece of music.

Sample rate The number of times an analogue to digital converter samples the signal every second, measured in Hertz (e.g. 44,100 times per second = 44.1kHz).

Sampler A device used to capture, edit, manipulate, store and playback **samples**.

Scratching A DJ performance technique: manually rotating a turntable platter while the needle is in contact with the vinyl to create a scratching sound.

Self-oscillation A phenomenon that occurs when the resonance value (or Q) has been set so high that a filter will generate a tone on its own.

Sequence 1) A piece of music input by means of a MIDI-capable device into a computer package which allows subsequent editing of almost every aspect of the MIDI data.

2) The immediate repetition of a musical motif at a higher or lower pitch.

Sequencer The computer package/hardware device used to facilitate the input and editing of **MIDI** data. Most sequencers are capable of combining MIDI data and audio and are called audio sequencers.

Side-chain A portion of the main signal that is separated out to be processed in some way. Some processors (such as compressors) use the side-chain to control when they act.

Signal-to-noise ratio The level of wanted signal compared to the level of unwanted noise.

Spot mic The technique of focussing a microphone on an individual or small group within a larger group that is being captured by other microphones so as to allow for selective boosting of the individual or group.

Staccato Italian for 'detached': a note that is noticeably separated from its neighbours.

Stereo Stereophonic: A signal carried on two channels, left and right, to represent a sound image as it might be picked up by two ears.

Stompbox A floor-mounted guitar effects unit, commonly called a 'pedal'.

Sync Short for 'synchronised': a system for keeping two or more pieces of equipment in time with each other.

Syncopation Placing strong beats where the pulse would normally dictate a weak beat, and/or weak beats where strong ones would be expected. Syncopation can occur on the beat, for example where the stress occurs on beats two and four when it would have been expected on beats one and three. It can also occur off the beat.

Tape saturation The point at which the magnetic particles on a tape will no longer respond to magnetic force. This has a subtle distortion effect that some artists find pleasing to the ear.

Tempo How fast or slow music is played; the speed of the music. Indicated at the start of a piece by a word (such as 'fast' or 'moderate') or a metronome marking.

Texture The sound quality of a piece, dependent on such features as the number of parts, the tone quality of the instruments and/or voices, and the spacing between the parts.

Theremin An early synthesiser played by means of moving the hands in proximity to one or two aerials.

Threshold A preset loudness point which, once passed, causes a process to occur. Used in, for example, compressors and gates.

Timbre The precise tone quality of a particular instrument, part or noise element in music. It may include a description of the speed of the attack and decay of the sound, the nature of the elements that make up the sound (such as particular waveforms) and subjective opinions on the quality of the tone.

Tonewheel A series of disks rotated by a motor in proximity to an electromagnetic pickup.

Tremolo arm A metal arm (colloquially referred to as 'whammy bar') attached to the bridge of a guitar that enables the user to change the tension of the strings, altering the pitch of the sounding note(s).

Triggering To cause an event to begin. To trigger a sample is to start the sample playing.

Turntablism The art of using one or more turntables combined with a DJ mixer to manipulate and mix sounds – using the turntable as an instrument.

Valve amplifiers Amplifiers that use vacuum tubes (valves) instead of transistors in the pre-amp and/or power amp stages. These are often felt to give a 'warmer' sound.

Violining A guitar playing technique: a note is struck while the volume control is at its lowest value and is then immediately turned up. This results in the loss of the attack portion of the note.

Virtual modelling Creating a software version of a hardware device.